Reykjavik Travel Guide with Detai

Welcome to Reykjavik: Your Gateway to Iceland's Enchanting Capital

Welcome to Reykjavik, the vibrant and captivating capital city of Iceland. Nestled on the edge of the North Atlantic Ocean, Reykjavik is a city that seamlessly blends natural beauty, rich history, innovative design, and a thriving cultural scene. With its picturesque landscapes, bustling streets, and warm-hearted locals, Reykjavik offers an unforgettable experience for every traveler.

Discover Reykjavik's Rich History: Uncover the intriguing stories of Reykjavik's past as you explore its historical landmarks, from the ancient settlement sites to the charming old town. Immerse yourself in the fascinating tales of Vikings, sagas, and the country's struggle for independence, all of which have shaped the unique identity of Iceland.

Experience a Thriving Arts and Culture Scene: Reykjavik is a haven for art enthusiasts, with its numerous museums, galleries, and street art that breathe life into the city's streets. Immerse yourself in the vibrant cultural scene by attending live performances, visiting contemporary art exhibitions, and indulging in the local music, literature, and film festivals that showcase Iceland's creative spirit.

Savor Culinary Delights: Reykjavik's burgeoning food scene offers a delightful fusion of traditional Icelandic cuisine and innovative culinary creations. From hearty seafood dishes to unique local delicacies, embark on a gastronomic journey that reflects the country's rich natural resources and the creativity of its chefs.

Don't forget to indulge in the renowned Icelandic hot dog and sample the world-famous Icelandic skyr.

Marvel at Natural Wonders: Reykjavik serves as a gateway to the breathtaking natural wonders that define Iceland's landscape. Witness the ethereal beauty of the Northern Lights dancing across the Arctic sky, soak in the therapeutic waters of geothermal hot springs, and explore the majestic glaciers, waterfalls, and geysers that dot the surrounding countryside.

Embrace the Spirit of Adventure: Whether you're a nature lover, an outdoor enthusiast, or an adrenaline junkie, Reykjavik offers a wealth of exhilarating activities. Embark on thrilling glacier hikes, embark on whale watching expeditions, go horseback riding on Icelandic horses, or take a thrilling snowmobile ride across icy landscapes. The possibilities for adventure are endless.

This comprehensive travel guide will be your trusted companion as you navigate the wonders of Reykjavik. From detailed insights into top attractions and hidden gems to practical information on transportation, accommodation, dining, and more, we are here to help you make the most of your journey.

So, pack your bags, embrace the spirit of exploration, and get ready to embark on an unforgettable adventure in Reykjavik, where nature's wonders meet cultural treasures, creating an experience unlike any other. Welcome to the enchanting world of Reykjavik, the gateway to Iceland's captivating capital!

Contents

Reykjavik - Travel Guide 1

1. Introduction 6
    1.1 Overview of Reykjavik 6
    1.2 History of Reykjavik 7
    1.3 Culture and People 9
    1.4 General Travel Information 10
    1.5 Top Tips for Traveling to Reykjavik 10
    1.6 Budget saving tips 11
    1.7 The most Useful apps to Download 12
2. Getting There and Around 14
    2.1 By Air 14
    2.2 By Sea 14
    2.3 Public Transportation 14
    2.4 How to Get from the Airport to the Center of Reykjavik 16
3. Accommodation 17
    3.1 Luxury Hotels 17
    3.2 Mid-range Hotels 17
    3.3 Budget Hotels and Hostels 17
    3.4 Self-catering and Vacation Rentals 17
    3.5 Unique Accommodation Options 18
4. Food and Drink 19
    4.1 Icelandic Cuisine Overview 19
    4.2 Fine Dining 20
    4.3 Casual Dining 20
    4.4 Street Food and Quick Bites 20
    4.5 Vegetarian and Vegan Options 21
    4.6 Local Delicacies to Try 21
    4.7 Best Cafes and Bars 22
    4.8 Our favorite Dining Places in Reykjavik 22
5. Sightseeing in Reykjavik 25
    5.1 Historical Landmarks 25
    5.2 Museums and Galleries 28

3

5.3 Parks and Outdoor Spaces 30

5.4 Churches and Architectural Wonders 30

5.5 Nearby Natural Wonders 31

5.6 Tours and Excursions 32

6. Shopping 33

6.1 Shopping Centers and Malls 33

6.2 Local Markets 33

6.3 Souvenir and Specialty Shops 33

6.4 Icelandic Design and Fashion Stores 33

7. Nightlife 35

7.1 Clubs and Live Music Venues 35

7.2 Pubs and Bars 35

7.3 Cultural Performances and Shows 35

7.4 Festivals and Events 36

8. Outdoor Activities and Adventure 37

8.1 Hiking and Walking Trails 37

8.2 Water Sports 37

8.3 Whale and Puffin Watching 37

8.4 Northern Lights Viewing 38

8.5 Hot Springs and Geothermal Pools 38

9. Health and Safety 40

9.1 Health and Medical Facilities 40

9.2 Safety Tips and Emergency Numbers 40

9.3 Accessibility for Travelers with Disabilities 40

10. Travel Tips and Cultural Etiquette 42

10.1 Currency, Credit Cards, and Tipping 42

10.2 Internet and Connectivity 42

10.3 Cultural Norms and Etiquette 42

10.4 Icelandic Language Basics 42

11. Seasonal Guide 44

11.1 Summer in Reykjavik 44

11.2 Winter in Reykjavik 44

11.3 Best Time to Visit 44

- 12. Itineraries 45
  - 12.1 One-day Itinerary 45
  - 12.2 Three-day Itinerary 46
  - 12.3 One-week Itinerary 47
  - 12.4 Special Interest Itineraries 48
- 13. Beyond Reykjavik 50
  - 13.1 Golden Circle 50
  - 13.2 South Coast 54
  - 13.3 Westfjords 57
  - 13.4 The Icelandic Highlands 61
- 14. Three-Day Detailed Itinerary 63
  - 1st Day In Reykjavik - Itinerary 63
  - 1st Day in Reykjavik - Map 66
  - ZoomTip 1.1: Thingvellir National Park 66
  - ZoomTip 1.2: The Great Geysir 67
  - ZoomTip 1.3: Gullfoss Waterfalls 68
  - 2nd Day In Reykjavik – Itinerary 69
  - 2nd Day in Reykjavik - Map 71
  - ZoomTip 2.1: Blue Lagoon geothermal spa 71
  - ZoomTip 2.2: Snaefellsjokull National Park 72
  - 3rd Day In Reykjavik – Itinerary 74
  - 3rd Day in Reykjavik – Map 75
  - ZoomTip 3.1: Hallgrímskirkja Church 76
- Thank You! 78
- Copyright Notice 79

1. Introduction

Welcome to the vibrant, lively city of Reykjavik - the capital and cultural heartbeat of Iceland. Situated on the southwestern coast of the country, Reykjavik offers a remarkable blend of rich history, unique culture, modern design, and raw natural beauty that is sure to leave any traveler spellbound.

Despite its small size, Reykjavik is packed with countless things to explore, including world-class museums, bustling local markets, charming coffee houses, exciting nightlife, and scenic outdoor spaces. But what truly sets this city apart is its warm, hospitable people and its proximity to some of the most magnificent natural wonders in the world.

Whether you're planning to stay within the city limits or use it as a base for exploring the greater part of Iceland, this comprehensive guide aims to provide all the information and tips you'll need to make your journey an unforgettable experience.

1.1 Overview of Reykjavik

Reykjavik, meaning *'Smokey Bay,'* is not just Iceland's capital and largest city, but also the world's northernmost capital. With a population of approximately 130,000 inhabitants in the city and about 230,000 in the Capital Region, Reykjavik might feel like a small town, but it certainly packs a punch.

Its prime location on the Faxa Bay brings stunning ocean views and an abundance of wildlife, with regular sightings of whales and bird species, particularly during the warmer months. Despite the city's relatively short existence - a little over 200 years - Reykjavik has transformed into a modern, vibrant city known for its commitment to renewable energy, safety, cleanliness, and high quality of life.

The city's heart is characterized by **colorful Nordic houses**, and its skyline is dominated by the impressive *Hallgrímskirkja* church. Art and culture are woven into the fabric of life in Reykjavik, with a plethora of galleries, museums, and cultural events happening throughout the year.

The city's energy is reflected in its lively nightlife scene, fueled by the famous Icelandic beer. But it's not just the party scene that excites visitors - the city's food scene is rapidly growing, with numerous restaurants serving everything from traditional Icelandic dishes to international cuisine.

Furthermore, Reykjavik serves as a gateway to the stunning Icelandic wilderness. From here, you can embark on various tours and excursions, such as the Golden Circle route, the Blue Lagoon, and even expeditions to see the enchanting Northern Lights.

Welcome to Reykjavik – a city where the warmth of the people is contrasted only by the coolness of its surrounding landscape, where the old meets the new, and where each day brings forth a new opportunity for adventure.

1.2 History of Reykjavik

When it comes to a comprehensive overview of Reykjavik's history, it's not just the story of a city, but rather, the narrative of a nation.

The Settlement Era

The history of Reykjavik begins around the year 874 AD, when Norse chieftain Ingólfur Arnarson and his wife Hallveig are said to have become the first permanent Norse settlers on the island. Their journey from Norway to Iceland, as chronicled in the *Landnámabók* ('The Book of Settlements'), established Reykjavik's roots in the Age of Settlements. The name Reykjavik, meaning 'Smoky Bay,' was supposedly given due to the geothermal steam rising from the ground, creating a smoky illusion.

Throughout the early settlement era, Reykjavik was predominantly a farmstead, with the area providing ideal conditions for farming and fishing. During these times, Iceland was divided into chieftains, each operating independently, with the area of Reykjavik coming under the jurisdiction of the Kjalarnes Chieftain.

Middle Ages to Early Modern Era

From the middle ages to the early modern period, Reykjavik remained a largely agricultural society, with little in terms of urban development. However, the history of Reykjavik, and indeed all of Iceland, changed dramatically in the 13th century with the onset of what is known as the *Age of the Sturlungs* - a violent period of civil war and power struggles among the chieftains.

During the 13th and 14th centuries, Icelandic society experienced numerous changes, culminating in the loss of independence to Norway in 1262. This was followed by a shift to Danish rule in the 14th century following the Kalmar Union, which united the Scandinavian countries under a single monarch.

17th Century to 19th Century

By the 17th and 18th centuries, the Danish Crown had a monopoly over Icelandic trade, leading to significant economic hardship for Icelanders. It wasn't until the late 18th century that change began to occur. In 1786, Reykjavik was granted municipal charter status, making it one of the six communities in Iceland with trading rights. This decision marked a significant turning point in Reykjavik's history as it led to the town's urban development.

The late 19th century brought forth a renewed sense of Icelandic nationalism, catalyzed by the Romantic movement sweeping through Europe. Jón Sigurðsson emerged as a prominent leader during this period, advocating for Icelandic independence.

20th Century and Beyond

The 20th century marked significant milestones in the growth and development of Reykjavik. In 1904, Reykjavik elected its first mayor, marking the advent of modern political organization. The city expanded rapidly in the years following World War II, transforming from a small town into a bustling capital.

On June 17, 1944, in the wake of World War II and the withdrawal of British and American troops, Iceland officially became an independent republic. This date holds special significance for Reykjavik, as the city was the epicenter of the independence movement, and the ceremony was held at Þingvellir, not far from the city.

In the years since independence, Reykjavik has seen continued development and progress. The city hosted the world-famous Fischer vs. Spassky chess match in 1972, and in 1986, the Reykjavik Summit between Ronald Reagan and Mikhail Gorbachev marked a turning point in ending the Cold War.

Present-day Reykjavík is a thriving metropolis with a growing population and economy. The city's past is beautifully interwoven into its present, with historical sites like the *National Museum of Iceland* and the *Arbaer Open Air Museum* preserving and showcasing its rich heritage.

The **20th century** also saw the implementation of geothermal energy in Reykjavik, a hallmark of its modern infrastructure. Today, the city is powered primarily by renewable energy, a testament to Iceland's commitment to sustainable development and an integral part of Reykjavik's identity.

Furthermore, the *Harpa Concert Hall*, completed in 2011, symbolizes Reykjavik's progress in recent years. This modern architectural masterpiece on the harbor is a vibrant cultural and social center, playing host to a myriad of events including concerts, conferences, and exhibitions.

From Economic Crisis to Tourism Boom

The 2008 economic crisis hit Reykjavik hard, causing a collapse of the banking system and leading to considerable economic and political instability. However, the crisis eventually resulted in a shift in the country's economic focus, leading to a significant boost in tourism. Low-cost air travel, the city's natural and cultural attractions, and Iceland's unique location between North America and Europe have since made Reykjavik a popular tourist destination.

Today, the history of Reykjavik continues to unfold. The city is growing and evolving while preserving its unique charm, history, and cultural heritage. It stands as a beacon of sustainability, resilience, and creativity, reflecting both the trials and triumphs of its past. Reykjavik is not only a testament to the spirit of the Icelandic people but also a model of innovation and sustainability for cities around the world.

This mix of the old and new, the traditional and the innovative, is perhaps what makes Reykjavik's history so captivating. As you walk the streets of this city, you don't just observe its history - you experience it, live it, and become a part of it.

Whether it's exploring the traditional turf houses, sampling the local cuisine, or bathing in a geothermal pool under the Northern Lights, the history of Reykjavik is waiting for you to explore. So get ready to step back in time and forward into the future as you journey through Reykjavik, a city that's as rich in its history as it is in its appeal.

1.3 Culture and People
The People of Reykjavik

The people of Reykjavik, like those of Iceland in general, are known for their **warmth, resilience, and hospitable nature**. With a population of just over 130,000, the city exudes a small-town charm, with a close-knit community that's proud of its heritage and welcoming to visitors.

Despite the small population, there's a rich diversity within the city, with many nationalities and cultures represented. Most residents are of Icelandic descent, but there's also a growing community of immigrants, particularly from Poland, Lithuania, and the Philippines.

The people of Reykjavik are generally fluent in English, besides their native Icelandic. They're also highly educated, with a high literacy rate and a strong emphasis on creativity and innovation. Iceland, as a whole, has a very low crime rate and Reykjavik is one of the safest capital cities in the world.

The Culture of Reykjavik

The culture of Reykjavik is a blend of traditional and contemporary, with deep roots in Norse heritage coupled with a thriving modern arts scene. The city is a haven for art lovers, with numerous galleries, museums, and street art that add color and life to its streets.

Literature plays a significant role in Icelandic culture, reflecting the nation's title as a "Land of the Sagas". Icelanders are known for their high literacy rate and love for books. The capital city embraces this tradition with various bookstores and libraries, including the National Library of Iceland. The city also celebrates the annual Reykjavik International Literary Festival, a must-visit for any literary enthusiast.

Music is another integral part of Reykjavik's culture. It's the birthplace of internationally acclaimed artists like Björk and Of Monsters and Men. The city offers a vibrant music scene, from the church hall performances to the Harpa Concert Hall, and the various music festivals like Iceland Airwaves and Secret Solstice.

Reykjavik's culinary culture has been evolving, too. There's a growing interest in using locally sourced and seasonal ingredients. From high-end dining to the city's hot dog stands, there's a culinary experience for everyone.

A unique aspect of Reykjavik's culture is the locals' belief in the supernatural, such as elves and trolls, which are often featured in local folklore and traditions. While not everyone believes in these mythical beings, they play a significant role in the country's cultural identity.

1.4 General Travel Information

Entry Requirements: Travelers from the EU/EEA, the UK, and the Schengen Area do not need a visa to visit Iceland for stays of up to 90 days. Non-EU/EEA travelers may need a visa depending on their home country, so check with the Icelandic Directorate of Immigration or your local embassy for details.

Currency: The official currency is the Icelandic Króna (ISK). While some places accept Euros or US Dollars, it's not widespread. Credit and debit cards are widely accepted, including in taxis and even some vending machines.

Weather: Reykjavik has a subpolar oceanic climate, with cool summers and relatively mild winters for its latitude. The weather can change rapidly, so it's best to pack layers and be prepared for anything.

Best Time to Visit: The best time to visit Reykjavik depends on what you want to see and do. The summer months (June to August) offer the Midnight Sun and warmer temperatures, ideal for hiking and exploring. The winter months (November to February) offer a chance to see the Northern Lights.

Language: The official language is Icelandic, but English is widely spoken and understood. Icelandic is a challenging language to learn, but locals appreciate any attempts to speak it!

Health and Safety: Reykjavik is very safe, with low crime rates. Tap water is safe to drink, and healthcare facilities are excellent, but health insurance is recommended as medical costs can be high for non-residents.

Electricity: Iceland uses Type F power outlets, and the standard voltage is 230 V. Travelers from countries using different voltages or plugs will need an adapter or converter.

Internet and Telecommunications: Wi-Fi is widely available, and Iceland offers good mobile coverage. The country code is +354.

Remember, each country's Covid-19 entry and exit requirements can change without notice. Be sure to check the latest rules and regulations before your trip.

1.5 Top Tips for Traveling to Reykjavik

#1: **Reykjavik is a very expensive city,** and so is the rest of Iceland as well. You should probably follow some of the advice we provide in this guide for not spending a fortune on your three days visit to Reykjavik, but you will still need some money for coming here since nothing is cheap.

#2: **Try to visit Reykjavik during summertime**: consider June, July or August as the best months for visiting Iceland. Yes, it's true that you won't be able to see the gorgeous northern lights during this time of the year, which is a real shame, but the weather is much nicer and will let you enjoy the most out of Iceland. During the rest of the year the weather in Iceland is harsh, and sometimes it does not allow you to do any sightseeing or outdoor activity at all.

#3: **Bring layers of clothes**. Even if you come during the summer, when the weather is much better, you will still need to think about the clothes you bring to Iceland. The weather is very unpredictable and can change many times within the same day. And the wind in Iceland is probably different from everything you know: it can be incredibly strong at times, so a good wind and raincoat is a must, no matter when you're visiting the country.

#4: **Rent a car**. There are two ways of going back and forth to the most amazing spots near Reykjavik: renting a car and driving yourself or taking tours from Reykjavik. In this travel guide, we recommend the car option, especially if you're more than two people traveling. The main reasons are that in this way you are free to go to these places whenever you want and stay at them for as much time as you feel like.

#5: **Don't limit yourself to the famous touristic spots only**. In this guide we will recommend some specific unusual places in Iceland, and you will also find information about some others while you are in Reykjavik, but you should know that Iceland is one amazing place and you will find astonishingly beautiful places and landscapes just wherever you go, even if you decide to go in any random direction. So, if you go for the renting a car option, it's a good plan just to use a morning or an afternoon to drive wherever you want to, and you'll see that you will find amazing landscapes with no tourists at all, and no local people neither. It's an excellent way to experience that feeling of isolation that characterizes Iceland so well.

1.6 Budget saving tips

If you're coming to Iceland, then it's very likely you've already heard stories about how expensive it is. And unfortunately we have to confirm that this is true: it's one of the most expensive countries in the world. However, if you follow some easy guidelines, you will be able to enjoy your visit without spending your entire monthly salary in just a few days! Here are some of the tips we recommend:

1- **Don't take taxis** unless it's necessary. Yes, not taking taxis is always a good way of saving some money while traveling anywhere, but this statement applies in particular in Reykjavik, where taxi fares are expensive.
2- **Try to rent a car** and do the Golden Circle and the rest of the attractions near Reykjavik on your own rather than taking tours from Reykjavik. This option is even more convenient if you are traveling in a group of 3 people or more but maybe does not apply if you are going alone.
3- If you're coming in Summer, **consider doing some camping!** If the weather is not bad, camping in the middle of volcanoes, glaciers or lava fields is simply excellent and will save you lots of money.
4- If you're coming in Winter or you simply don't like camping, **consider staying in shared dormitories in hostels instead of traditional hotels**. We know that sharing the same room with other people is not the best when you're trying to get some good sleep, but the differences in prices are enormous. You will be able to get a bed in a shared room for between 35€ to 50€, while the cheapest double room in a hotel in Reykjavik costs around 150€.
5- **Always try to buy groceries in supermarkets and cook your meals**. Going out for lunch or dinner in Reykjavik is also extremely expensive. Any regular restaurant costs more than 50€ per person; so if you simply buy some basic stuff in a supermarket (preferably **Bónus,** which is the cheapest one) will allow you to save a lot of money. However, restaurants in Reykjavik are mostly excellent, despite their high prices, so you can consider going out for dinner for one special occasion in your holidays. We will go deeper into this next in the *"Our favorite dining places in Reykjavik"* section.

1. 7 The most Useful apps to Download

When you're preparing for a trip to Reykjavik, these apps will help you navigate the city, keep up with events, understand the weather, and even learn a little Icelandic.

1. Strætó
The official app for Reykjavik's bus system allows you to plan your journey, see where your bus is in real-time, and even buy tickets directly from your phone.

Download: iOS, Android
Website: www.straeto.is

2. Appy Hour
This app by the Reykjavik Grapevine lists all the best happy hour deals in the city, so you'll never be short of places to get a discount drink.

Download: iOS, Android
Website: www.grapevine.is/appy-hour

3. Veður
Created by the Icelandic Meteorological Office, this app provides detailed and reliable weather forecasts for all areas of Iceland, including severe weather alerts.

Download: iOS, Android
Website: www.vedur.is

4. Tjalda
If you're planning to camp during your stay, Tjalda is invaluable. It lists all campsites in Iceland, their facilities, prices, and opening times.

Download: iOS, Android
Website: www.tjalda.is/en/

5. 112 Iceland
The official app of the Icelandic emergency services allows you to send an SMS with your location to the 112 emergency number if you're in trouble.

Download: iOS, Android
Website: www.safetravel.is/112-iceland-app

6. Icelandic
If you want to try your hand at the local language, this app is a comprehensive guide to Icelandic, including pronunciation.

Download: iOS, Android
Website: N/A

7. Wapp - Walking app
This app offers numerous walking and hiking routes, providing trail maps, difficulty levels, and points of interest for each route.

Download: iOS, Android
Website: www.wapp.is

8. Reykjavik City App
Official guide to Reykjavik with information about events, restaurants, attractions, and much more.

Download: iOS, Android
Website: www.visitreykjavik.is/reykjavik-app

By having these apps on your mobile device, you'll be well-prepared to make the most of your visit to Reykjavik.

2. Getting There and Around

Getting to Reykjavik and moving around the city can be a seamless experience. Here's what you need to know:

2.1 By Air

The main gateway to Reykjavik and indeed Iceland is through the Keflavik International Airport (KEF), located approximately 50 km southwest of the city. The airport is served by various international airlines, with regular flights to and from several European and North American cities.

Once you land, you can get to Reykjavik city center by airport shuttle services, taxis, or rental cars. The Flybus and the Gray Line Airport Express are two reliable shuttle services, operating in sync with the flight schedule. The ride to the city takes about 45 minutes.

For domestic flights within Iceland, Reykjavik Airport, located in the city center, is the main hub.

2.2 By Sea

Another way to reach Reykjavik is by sea. Various cruise ships dock at Reykjavik's harbor during the summer months. The city also has a ferry connection with the Faroe Islands and Denmark, operated by Smyril Line. Once docked, most of the city's attractions are within walking distance from the port.

2.3 Public Transportation

Getting around Reykjavik is relatively straightforward, thanks to its excellent public transportation system.

City Buses (Strætó bs):
Reykjavik's primary public transportation is its extensive bus network. Strætó bs runs numerous routes across the city and its suburbs, with service starting around 6:30 AM and ending just after midnight. On weekends and public holidays, the frequency of buses is reduced.

A single ride ticket costs ISK 470 (as of 2023, subject to change) and can be purchased directly from the bus driver or in advance at selected stores, but it is recommended to download the Strætó app. The app provides route maps, real-time bus tracking, ticket purchase, and even free onboard Wi-Fi passwords. Note that the bus drivers do not provide change, so exact fare is necessary if purchasing on board. For regular users, there are also day passes, three-day passes, and week passes available.

Website: www.straeto.is
App: Strætó (Available on both iOS and Android)

Taxi Services:

Taxis in Reykjavik are reliable and operate on a metered system. They can be booked in advance, hailed on the street, or picked up from designated taxi ranks. There are a few taxi services such as Hreyfill taxi service and BSR taxi service. Most of the taxis have card machines, and they accept both credit cards and debit cards.

Websites: www.hreyfill.is (Hreyfill), www.bsr.is (BSR)

Bicycle Rental:

Reykjavik is a bike-friendly city, with numerous cycle paths and bike rental services available, such as Reykjavik Bike Tours and WOW City Bike. Prices for bike rental vary but expect to pay around ISK 2,500 for a half-day rental and ISK 4,000 for a full day. Many services also offer guided bike tours, which can be a great way to see the city and learn about its history and culture.

Websites: www.icelandbike.com (Reykjavik Bike Tours), www.wowcitybike.com (WOW City Bike)

Car Rental:

Numerous car rental companies operate in Reykjavik, including international chains and local providers such as Blue Car Rental and Geysir. Prices vary widely depending on the car and time of year, but expect to pay from around ISK 5,000 per day for a small car. Keep in mind that parking in the city center may incur charges, and it's essential to familiarize yourself with Icelandic driving laws before you set off.

Websites: www.bluecarrental.is (Blue Car Rental), www.geysir.is (Geysir Car Rental)

Walking:

Given its compact size, many of Reykjavik's key attractions can easily be reached on foot. The city is pedestrian-friendly, with plenty of signages and pedestrian zones. An interactive map of Reykjavik, available on the Visit Reykjavik website, can help you plan your route.

Website: www.visitreykjavik.is/city/map (Visit Reykjavik Map)

2.4 How to Get from the Airport to the Center of Reykjavik

Keflavik International Airport (KEF)

Keflavik International Airport is located 50 km southwest of Reykjavik. It's a 40-minute drive to get to downtown Reykjavik from the airport.

If you are not renting a car at the airport and driving to the city, there are several different options you can choose for this trip. The most popular option is to take the FlyBus, which is a bus that departs from right outside the airport exactly 40 minutes after the arrival of each flight. The tickets for this bus cost 2.500 ISK (20,50€) and can be purchased at the airport or online through the Flybus website.

Another option, which is the most used by Icelanders is to take the regular public bus n°55 (Straetó). The price is lower, 1.600 ISK (around 13€), but it takes a little longer, about 70 minutes from the airport to the center of the city, compared to the 40 minutes of the Flybus option. You can check the timetable at the Straetó website: there are nine buses every day from the airport to Reykjavik.

The last and most expensive option is to take a taxi, which we do not recommend due to the excessive price. A taxi from Keflavik International Airport to the center of Reykjavik costs around 17.500 ISK (150€).

3. Accommodation

Reykjavik boasts a variety of accommodations to suit all budgets and tastes. Whether you're looking for luxury hotels, budget-friendly hostels, or unique accommodations, the city has something to offer.

3.1 Luxury Hotels

For travelers seeking a luxurious stay, Reykjavik offers a variety of high-end hotels:

- **Hotel Borg by Keahotels:** Overlooking the beautiful Austurvöllur square in the heart of Reykjavik, Hotel Borg offers elegance, luxury, and top-notch service. Prices start from 35,000 ISK per night. Website: Hotel Borg
- **Canopy by Hilton Reykjavik City Centre:** This hotel merges modern design with historic charm. The hotel offers spacious rooms, a fitness center, and a complimentary evening tasting of local beverages and spirits. Prices start at approximately 35,000 ISK per night. Website:

3.2 Mid-range Hotels

There are also numerous mid-range hotels that offer excellent services at a more affordable price:

- **CenterHotel Midgardur:** Located on Reykjavik's main shopping street, this hotel provides comfortable rooms, a Nordic-style breakfast, and a spa. Prices start around 20,000 ISK per night. Website: CenterHotel Midgardur
- **Skuggi Hotel by Keahotels:** This hotel offers a minimalistic and modern design inspired by Icelandic nature. Prices start from 15,000 ISK per night. Website:

3.3 Budget Hotels and Hostels

For the budget-conscious traveler, Reykjavik offers several hostels and budget hotels:

- **Kex Hostel:** Located in an old biscuit factory, Kex offers dormitory rooms and private rooms at budget prices. A bed in a dormitory starts from 3,000 ISK. Website: Kex Hostel
- **Reykjavik City HI Hostel:** A budget-friendly, eco-certified hostel offering a variety of room types. Prices for a bed in a dormitory start from 2,500 ISK. Website:

3.4 Self-catering and Vacation Rentals

For travelers who prefer self-catering options, there are plenty of vacation rentals available:

- **Reykjavik4You Apartments:** These apartments are located in the city center and fully equipped for self-catering. Prices start from 20,000 ISK per night for a one-bedroom apartment. Website: [Reykjavik4You](#)
- **Stay Apartments Einholt:** Affordable apartments with a fully equipped kitchen, located near the downtown area. Prices start from 10,000 ISK per night. Website:

3.5 Unique Accommodation Options

For a truly unique stay, consider these options:

- **ION City Hotel:** This design hotel blends modern design with sustainable practices and offers a panoramic view of the city. Prices start from 30,000 ISK per night. Website: [ION City Hotel](#)
- **Tower Suites Reykjavik:** For a room with a view, consider these suites located in one of the city's tallest buildings, offering panoramic views of the city, sea, and mountains. Prices start at 45,000 ISK per night. Website: [Tower Suites](#)

Before booking, it's always good to check on the accommodation's policies regarding cancellations, check-in/check-out times, and included amenities. Prices may also vary depending on the season and availability, so book in advance if you're traveling during the high season (summer months) or during major events or festivals.

4. Food and Drink

Embarking on a culinary journey is an essential part of exploring Reykjavik. The city offers a mix of traditional and contemporary dishes, making it an exciting destination for food lovers.

4.1 Icelandic Cuisine Overview

Icelandic cuisine has evolved over the centuries, influenced by the island's isolation and harsh climate. It's characterized by its unique ingredients, drawn from the sea, the land, and the air.

Seafood and Lamb: Being an island, seafood is a staple in Icelandic cuisine. You can find fresh fish like cod, haddock, and plaice on most restaurant menus. Reykjavik's harbor is the perfect place to savor the catch of the day. Similarly, due to Iceland's vast pastures and low population, lamb is also very popular. The lamb in Iceland is considered exceptionally pure and flavorful due to the animals' free-range, grass-fed lifestyle.

Fermented and Smoked Dishes: Icelandic cuisine also includes a variety of fermented and smoked dishes, a tradition born out of the necessity for preserving food through the long winter months. Þorramatur is a selection of traditional Icelandic food that includes fermented shark (hákarl), sheep's head (svið), and pickled ram's testicles (hrútspungar).

Dairy: Dairy products are a big part of the Icelandic diet. Skyr, a thick, yogurt-like dairy product, has been part of Icelandic cuisine for over a thousand years. It's often served with sugar, fruit, or berries and can be found in almost every grocery store and cafe in Reykjavik.

Rye Bread (Rúgbrauð): Another staple of Icelandic cuisine, rye bread, is a dark, dense bread that's traditionally baked in a pot or steamed in wooden casks by burying it in the ground near a hot spring.

Unique Delicacies: For the adventurous, there are dishes like puffin and minke whale. However, these are controversial due to conservation concerns. If you do choose to try these dishes, ensure they've been sourced sustainably.

Street Food: Reykjavik is famous for its hot dog (or pylsur) stands. The most famous one, Bæjarins Beztu Pylsur, often has a line but is worth the wait.

Icelandic Water: Don't forget to try the tap water! Icelandic tap water is incredibly pure, sourced from natural springs and requires no treatment.

Whether you're a foodie, a picky eater, or an adventurous eater, Reykjavik's diverse food scene ensures that there's something for everyone. From traditional Icelandic dishes to modern gastronomic experiences, the city's food scene invites you to take a delicious journey through its culture and history.

4.2 Fine Dining

Reykjavik offers an array of fine dining options, where chefs use local ingredients to create visually stunning and flavorful dishes. Here are a few options for upscale dining:

- **Dill Restaurant:** This was the first restaurant in Iceland to receive a Michelin star. Dill offers a set menu that changes weekly, showcasing fresh, local ingredients prepared with a modern twist. The restaurant is located in the Nordic House, and booking in advance is recommended. Prices for a 7-course meal start at 15,900 ISK, with a wine pairing option for an additional 11,900 ISK. Website: Dill
- **Grill Market (Grillmarkaðurinn):** Here, the chefs work closely with local farmers to get the best produce. They offer a variety of dishes including fish, lamb, and beef. The Grill Market is located in Lækjargata, in a beautifully decorated building. Website: Grillmarkaðurinn
- **Fish Market (Fiskmarkaðurinn):** This place serves a fusion of Icelandic and Japanese cuisine. The decor resembles an old Icelandic wooden house, which adds to the overall dining experience. Website:

4.3 Casual Dining

Casual dining in Reykjavik allows you to enjoy the city's culinary delights without breaking the bank. From hearty traditional dishes to modern street food, there's something for everyone:

- **Icelandic Street Food:** This family-run business is the first fast-food concept in Iceland with traditional Icelandic food. Here you can get affordable, hearty meals like lamb soup, fish stew, and pancakes. Website: Icelandic Street Food
- **Bæjarins Beztu Pylsur:** No visit to Reykjavik is complete without stopping at this iconic hot dog stand, which translates to "The Best Hot Dog in Town". It has been in operation since 1937 and has served the likes of Bill Clinton and the members of Metallica.
- **Fish and More (Sjavargrillid):** This place serves fresh seafood and vegan options in a cozy, casual setting. Website: Sjavargrillid
- **Hlemmur Food Hall (Hlemmur Mathöll):** This is the place to go if you want variety. The food hall is located in a former bus terminal and offers a range of food stalls serving everything from Vietnamese food to traditional Icelandic dishes and craft beer. Website:

4.4 Street Food and Quick Bites

Reykjavik is not only famous for its fine dining but also for its street food and quick bites. Here are some places you should consider for a fast, affordable, and delicious meal:

- **Bæjarins Beztu Pylsur:** Already mentioned earlier, but it's worth repeating. This hot dog stand is considered an institution in Reykjavik and is a must-visit. The hot dogs are made mostly from Icelandic lamb, along with pork and beef.
- **Noodle Station:** A perfect place to get a comforting bowl of noodle soup. Their soups come in three varieties: chicken, beef, and vegetable. Website: Noodle Station
- **Reykjavik Chips:** They serve the best Belgian-style fries in town, with a variety of sauces to choose from. Website: Reykjavik Chips
- **Valdís:** A popular ice cream parlor offering an array of flavors, including traditional and unusual ones such as licorice and blueberry Skyr. Website:

4.5 Vegetarian and Vegan Options

Reykjavik is also a city where vegetarians and vegans will feel at home. There's an impressive range of plant-based options available:

- **Glo Restaurant:** This place offers a variety of healthy options, with a menu that includes raw food dishes, vegan and vegetarian meals, and even gluten-free options. Website: Glo
- **Kaffi Vinyl:** This is an all-vegan restaurant and a popular spot for music lovers. They offer a variety of dishes and a selection of vinyl records to enjoy while you eat. Website: Kaffi Vinyl
- **Vinyl Bistro & Bar:** This plant-based restaurant offers an extensive menu of vegan and vegetarian options. Website: Vinyl Bistro & Bar
- **Garðurinn Ecstasy's Heart-Garden:** This small vegetarian café offers a different set menu each day, featuring dishes from around the world. It's an ideal place for a quick, healthy, and affordable lunch.

From traditional Icelandic delicacies to international cuisine, vegetarian, and vegan options, Reykjavik's food scene is sure to cater to all dietary needs and preferences.

4.6 Local Delicacies to Try

While in Reykjavik, it would be a miss not to try some of the local Icelandic delicacies. Here are a few unique local foods that you should consider:

- **Skyr:** This traditional Icelandic yogurt-like dairy product is a must-try. It's rich, creamy, and comes in various flavors. You can find Skyr in every supermarket and most restaurants.

- **Lamb:** Icelandic lamb has a unique and delicate flavor due to the animals' free-range lifestyle, grazing on wild grass, herbs, and berries.
- **Pylsur (Hot Dog):** You might think that hot dogs are an American thing, but Icelanders love their version, typically served with raw and fried onions, ketchup, sweet brown mustard, and a mayonnaise-based sauce with sweet relish.
- **Rúgbrauð (Rye Bread):** Traditionally baked using geothermal heat, this dense, dark bread has a slightly sweet flavor. It's delicious with Icelandic butter or topped with smoked salmon.
- **Hákarl (Fermented Shark):** This one's for the daring food explorers! This traditional dish is made from shark that's been fermented and hung to dry for several months. It's known for its strong ammonia-rich smell and acquired taste.

4.7 Best Cafes and Bars

Reykjavik has a thriving café culture and an energetic nightlife. Whether you are a coffee lover, beer enthusiast, or cocktail connoisseur, there's a place for you:

- **Reykjavik Roasters:** One of the city's best coffee shops, Reykjavik Roasters is known for its dedication to quality coffee. They source their beans directly from farmers and roast them in-house. Website: Reykjavik Roasters
- **Brauð & Co:** While technically a bakery, it's the perfect place to grab a coffee and one of their fabulous pastries or a slice of their famous cinnamon bread. Website: Brauð & Co
- **Mikkeller & Friends Reykjavik:** A must-visit for craft beer lovers. This stylish bar offers an extensive selection of beers on tap, including their own brews and guest beers. Website: Mikkeller & Friends
- **Slippbarinn:** Known as the first cocktail bar in Reykjavik, Slippbarinn offers an impressive list of cocktails made with a mix of international and local ingredients. It's located inside the Icelandair Hotel Reykjavik Marina. Website: Slippbarinn
- **Lebowski Bar:** This fun and quirky bar is themed after the movie "The Big Lebowski". They have a bowling alley and serve a variety of White Russian cocktails. Website: Lebowski Bar

4.8 Our favorite Dining Places in Reykjavik

As said before, going out for dinner in **Reykjavik** can be pretty expensive, but it's worth it to do it at least one time. Iceland is now worldwide famous thanks to its amazing and unique landscapes, full of lava fields, volcanoes, glaciers, and all kinds of mountains, but very few people know that gastronomy is another one of the strongest qualities of this beautiful island. Here we mention some of our **favorite dining places in Reykjavik**:

1- **Saegreifinn** *(Geirsgata 8)*:

This magnificent place combines traditional Icelandic food with fresh fish, and in a cozy and relaxed atmosphere. Inside it has three different rooms or spaces, and one terrace. Sometimes they even have local musicians performing on the ground floor of the restaurant. The place is decorated with hundreds of photos of old local fishers. Don't forget to try the lobster soup, which is the specialty and most famous dish at Saegreifinn. The prices here at much lower than in the restaurants in downtown Reykjavik. You can have dinner here with only $25 per person.

2- **Laekjarbrekka** (Laekjarbrekka Bankastraeti 2):

This black wooden house was built by a wealthy Danish businessman in 1830 and was originally a bakery store. It has been restored a few years ago and converted into a restaurant, maintaining its original looks and feelings. It has a bar on the top floor, perfect for having a drink before or after dinner. The food is amazingly good, mostly Icelandic traditional dishes, with house specialties such as lamb or lobster.

3- **Baejarnis Beztu** (Tryggvagata and Pósthússtraeti):

Hot dogs are incredibly popular in Iceland, and Baejarnis Beztu is a real institution when it comes to hot dogs. Situated in front of the bay, this place is legendary all across town and known for making the best hot dog in Iceland. Of course, this is not the most glamorous option for dinner in Reykjavik, but you'll be surprised by the quality of the hot dogs they serve, and, as you may suspect, the prices for eating here are much lower than at most other places in town.

4- **Fish Market** (Adalstraeti 12):

This place is rather new, but has already been established as one of the most interesting dining places in Reykjavik. A fish restaurant, it combines traditional Icelandic food with different Asian cooking techniques, resulting in a fascinating fusion. It's probably the best place in Iceland to taste the original Icelandic Sushi.

5. Sightseeing in Reykjavik

Reykjavik is a city that beautifully marries natural beauty with human-made attractions. From its modern architecture to its historical landmarks, the city offers a rich tapestry of experiences that appeal to all types of travelers.

5.1 Historical Landmarks

Reykjavik and the surrounding areas are steeped in history, and a visit to its historical landmarks will give you a glimpse into its rich past.

Hallgrímskirkja: This iconic church is one of the tallest structures in Iceland and offers a panoramic view of the city from its observation tower. Its unique design was inspired by the basalt lava flows of Iceland's landscape.

Harpa Concert Hall:

Harpa Concert Hall, located on the harbor in Reykjavik, is a cultural and architectural landmark of Iceland, celebrated for its stunning design and diverse array of performances.

Description:

Harpa Concert Hall and Conference Centre, inaugurated in 2011, stands out with its unique façade of geometric glass panels that shimmer in the light, reflecting both the sky and the surrounding harbor. The design is an impressive collaboration between Danish firm Henning Larsen Architects and renowned Icelandic-Danish artist Olafur Eliasson. The building is inspired by Iceland's rugged landscape and natural phenomena, such as the Northern Lights and basalt columns.

Inside Harpa, four concert halls and conference venues can accommodate a range of events. The largest hall, Eldborg, seats up to 1,800 people and is the main stage for the Icelandic Symphony Orchestra and the Icelandic Opera. The smaller halls - Norðurljós, Silfurberg, and Kaldalón - are versatile spaces used for various performances, including music concerts, theatre shows, conferences, and exhibitions.

Noteworthy Features:

1. The unique glass façade of Harpa changes colors with the lighting system and creates captivating reflections of the city and harbor, making it a beautiful sight day and night.

2. Inside, the halls boast state-of-the-art acoustics, designed by renowned acoustic designers Artec Consultants Inc, making for a superb listening experience.

3. Harpa is home to several bars and restaurants, including the ground-floor Smurstöðin, offering Icelandic tapas, and the top-floor Kolabrautin, providing panoramic views over Reykjavik.

4. Harpa is not just for concerts and conferences. The building is open to the public, and visitors can explore the building's unique architecture or enjoy the view from the upper levels.

Visiting Harpa:

Harpa is open to the public daily from 8:00 am to midnight. Guided tours in English are available, offering insights into the building's architecture, acoustics, and art, as well as a behind-the-scenes glimpse at concert preparations.

Address: Austurbakki 2, 101 Reykjavík, Iceland

Website: www.harpa.is

Whether you're attending a concert, exploring the building on a guided tour, or simply marveling at its stunning architecture from the outside, Harpa Concert Hall is an essential part of any visit to Reykjavik. Its fusion of art, culture, and architecture makes it a symbol of Reykjavik's creativity and resilience.

The Settlement Exhibition: Located in downtown Reykjavik, this museum showcases the archaeological remains of a Viking longhouse from the Settlement Age. Interactive displays provide insights into the lives of the first inhabitants of the city. Website: The Settlement Exhibition

Reykjavik Old Harbour: The Old Harbour area is one of the city's most picturesque and historic districts, dating back to the 20th century. Today, it's a vibrant area filled with restaurants, boutiques, and the departure point for whale-watching tours.

National Museum of Iceland:

The National Museum of Iceland (Þjóðminjasafn Íslands) is a captivating museum that tells the story of Iceland's rich history, from the Viking Age to the present day. Housed in a purpose-built modern building, the museum's exhibits offer a comprehensive exploration of Icelandic culture, heritage, and traditions.

Description:

The National Museum of Iceland is located in the heart of Reykjavik, near the University of Iceland. The museum showcases artifacts, archaeological discoveries, and multimedia presentations that provide a deep understanding of Iceland's past, offering a glimpse into the country's unique identity.

Top Exhibits to See:

1. **The Settlement Exhibition**: This permanent exhibition presents the remains of a Viking Age longhouse discovered during excavations in central Reykjavik. It provides a fascinating insight into the daily life of Iceland's early settlers.

2. **Medieval Iceland**: Explore the world of the Icelandic sagas, the captivating tales that chronicle the lives of the country's early inhabitants. The exhibit displays medieval manuscripts, archaeological finds, and cultural artifacts that highlight the importance of the sagas in shaping Icelandic identity.

3. **The Making of a Nation**: Journey through Iceland's history from the Middle Ages to the present day. Discover the struggles and triumphs of the Icelandic people, including their fight for independence and the development of a modern nation.

4. **From Poverty to Modernity**: This exhibit delves into the transformation of Icelandic society during the 19th and 20th centuries. Learn about the impact of industrialization, urbanization, and cultural changes on the country and its people.

5. **Viking Age Artefacts**: Marvel at the impressive collection of Viking Age artifacts, including weapons, tools, jewelry, and household items, which provide a glimpse into the lives of the early Icelandic settlers.

Visiting the National Museum:

The museum is open to the public from Tuesday to Sunday, 10:00 am to 5:00 pm. It's closed on Mondays. Guided tours are available, providing in-depth explanations of the exhibits and the history of Iceland.

Ticket Prices:

- Adults: ISK 2000

- Seniors (67+) and Disabled: ISK 1600

- Free admission for children and teenagers under 18

Address: Suðurgata 41, 101 Reykjavík, Iceland

Website: www.thjodminjasafn.is

Árbæjarsafn - The Open Air Museum: A little outside the city center, this open-air museum takes you back to the past, showing what life was like in Reykjavik in different eras. You can see traditional turf houses, a church, a school, and more. Website: Árbæjarsafn

Remember to check the websites for the most current information on opening hours and ticket prices. Exploring these historical landmarks will give you a better understanding of Reykjavik's history and the opportunity to marvel at its stunning architecture.

5.2 Museums and Galleries

Reykjavik is a city that celebrates art, culture, and history through a diverse range of museums and galleries. Here are some highlights:

Reykjavik Art Museum:

The Reykjavík Art Museum (Listasafn Reykjavíkur) is a leading art museum in Iceland and an essential destination for art lovers visiting Reykjavik.

Description:

Founded in 1973, the Reykjavík Art Museum is spread over three distinct locations in Reykjavik: Hafnarhús, Kjarvalsstaðir, and Ásmundarsafn. Each location offers a different perspective on Icelandic art.

Hafnarhús is located in the oldest part of Reykjavík, in a renovated warehouse by the old harbour. It houses modern and contemporary art collections and is home to the works of Erró, a prominent Icelandic pop artist.

Kjarvalsstaðir, named after the famous Icelandic painter Jóhannes S. Kjarval, showcases a vast collection of Kjarval's work, from his early pieces to his later, more abstract work. The museum also displays works by other Icelandic and international artists.

Ásmundarsafn is dedicated to the works of Ásmundur Sveinsson, a pioneer of Icelandic sculpture. The museum is housed in a unique building, designed and constructed largely by Sveinsson himself, serving as a testament to his innovative and artistic abilities.

Top Exhibits to See:

1. The Erró Collection at Hafnarhús: A vast collection of works by Erró, known as the "Picasso of Pop," offers a deep dive into the world of pop art.

2. The art of Jóhannes S. Kjarval at Kjarvalsstaðir: Kjarval's depictions of the Icelandic landscape and its people offer an insight into the heart of Iceland's culture and heritage.

3. The sculpture garden at Ásmundarsafn: Ásmundur Sveinsson's sculptures, influenced by both classic and modern styles, are displayed in the garden surrounding the museum.

Open Hours:

The museum's opening hours vary by location:

- Hafnarhús: Open daily from 10:00 - 17:00

- Kjarvalsstaðir: Open daily from 10:00 - 17:00

- Ásmundarsafn: Open from May to September from 10:00 - 17:00, and from October to April from 13:00 - 17:00

Ticket Prices:

Admission grants access to all three locations and is valid for 24 hours:

Adults: ISK 2000| Students, Senior Citizens (67+), Disabled: ISK 1000| Children under 18: Free

Address:

- Hafnarhús: Tryggvagata 17, 101 Reykjavík

- Kjarvalsstaðir: Flókagata 24, 105 Reykjavík

- Ásmundarsafn: Sigtún 105, 105 Reykjavík

Website: www.artmuseum.is

The Reykjavík Art Museum is not just a place to view art but an experience that offers a deep understanding of Iceland's vibrant art scene and cultural heritage. Whether you're an art aficionado or a casual visitor, the museum is a must-visit in Reykjavik.

The Einar Jónsson Museum: Dedicated to Iceland's first sculptor, this museum houses over 300 artworks. The sculpture garden outside is free to visit and open all year round. Website: [The Einar Jónsson Museum](#)

The Saga Museum: This museum recreates key moments in Icelandic history, offering a fascinating insight into the Icelandic sagas. The exhibits are lifelike silicone figures, created by one of the artists behind Yoda and the creatures in the Star Wars movies. Website: [The Saga Museum](#)

Icelandic Phallological Museum: Certainly one of the more unusual attractions, this museum hosts a collection of more than 200 penises and penile parts from almost all of the land and sea mammals found in Iceland. Website: [Icelandic Phallological Museum](#)

5.3 Parks and Outdoor Spaces

Reykjavik is known for its breathtaking natural beauty. The city has several parks and outdoor spaces where you can relax and enjoy nature:

- **Tjörnin (The Pond):** This small lake in the city center is home to various bird species. It's surrounded by parks and some of the city's main landmarks, including Reykjavik City Hall.
- **Hallargarður (Hallgrimskirkja Park):** Located at the foot of Hallgrímskirkja Church, this park is home to a statue of Leif Erikson, given to Iceland by the United States.
- **Laugardalur Park:** This is the city's main recreational area, with a zoo, botanical garden, swimming pool, sports facilities, and walking paths.
- **Elliðaárdalur Valley:** Just a short drive from the city center, this beautiful valley is crisscrossed by walking paths and bridleways. The Elliðaár river runs through the valley and is known for its salmon fishing.
- **Heiðmörk:** This nature reserve on the outskirts of the city is a popular spot for hiking, bird watching, and picnicking. It's also home to over 4 million trees, making it a great place to escape the bustle of the city.

Whether you are an art enthusiast or a nature lover, Reykjavik offers a variety of experiences to satisfy your interests. Be sure to take some time to explore the city's rich cultural offerings and beautiful outdoor spaces.

5.4 Churches and Architectural Wonders

Reykjavik is not only a city of stunning natural beauty, but it is also a place where architecture has taken on a life of its own, blending Nordic tradition with innovative design.

- **Hallgrímskirkja:** This has been mentioned before but deserves a second mention. As Reykjavik's main landmark, Hallgrímskirkja is an impressive Lutheran church standing 74.5 meters high, making it the tallest church in Iceland. The architecture was inspired by the natural basalt columns found throughout the country. Don't forget to take the elevator to the top for an unbeatable view of the city.
- **Harpa Concert Hall:** Another extraordinary example of Reykjavik's architectural prowess is the Harpa Concert Hall, located by the old harbor. With its distinctive honeycomb glass facade designed by artist Olafur Eliasson, Harpa beautifully reflects the surrounding seascape and sky.
- **Perlan (The Pearl):** This landmark building, situated on a hill overlooking Reykjavik, houses a planetarium, an exhibition about glaciers, and a revolving restaurant under its distinctive glass dome. The platform offers a fantastic 360° view of the city.
- **Sun Voyager Sculpture (Sólfar):** This stunning sculpture by Jón Gunnar Árnason is a dreamboat and an ode to the sun. Overlooking the sea, it's particularly beautiful at sunrise or sunset.
- **The Icelandic Opera:** Located in a modern, glass-covered building in midtown Reykjavik, it's home to a variety of performances from classic opera to contemporary productions.
- **Rauðhólar (The Red Hills):** Not a building but a natural architectural wonder within Reykjavik's city limits. These pseudo-craters were formed by volcanic activity, and their striking red and orange hues contrast beautifully with the surrounding greenery.

5.5 Nearby Natural Wonders

Iceland is known as the land of fire and ice due to its dramatic landscapes of volcanoes, glaciers, geysers, hot springs, lava fields, and waterfalls. Many of these natural wonders are easily accessible from Reykjavik.

- **Golden Circle:** This popular tourist route includes three stunning locations: the Þingvellir National Park, the Geysir geothermal area, and Gullfoss waterfall. Þingvellir is a UNESCO World Heritage site where the North American and Eurasian tectonic plates meet. Geysir is a geothermal area with bubbling mud pools and exploding geysers. Gullfoss, or the "Golden Falls," is one of the most impressive waterfalls in Iceland.

- **Blue Lagoon:** While technically man-made, the Blue Lagoon, with its geothermally heated mineral-rich waters, has become one of Iceland's most iconic natural attractions. Be sure to book in advance on their website: Blue Lagoon
- **Snaefellsnes Peninsula:** Often described as "Iceland in miniature," the Snaefellsnes Peninsula has a bit of everything: the Snaefellsjökull glacier, dramatic cliffs, black and golden sand beaches, volcanic craters, and charming fishing villages.
- **The South Coast:** Drive along the southern coast of Iceland to see stunning waterfalls like Seljalandsfoss and Skógafoss, the black sand beach of Reynisfjara, and the breathtaking cliffs of Dyrhólaey.
- **Vatnajökull National Park:** A bit further afield, but worth the trip for its extraordinary landscape. Home to the largest glacier in Europe, it also boasts Iceland's highest peak, Hvannadalshnúkur, and the stunning Jökulsárlón glacier lagoon.
- **Whale Watching Tours:** Leaving from Reykjavik's Old Harbor, these tours provide an opportunity to see some of the 20 different species of whale that can be found in Icelandic waters.

5.6 Tours and Excursions

There's plenty to explore in and around Reykjavik, and guided tours can provide a deeper understanding of the region's history, culture, and nature. Here are some highly recommended tours and excursions:

- **Golden Circle Tours:** A variety of companies offer day trips to the Golden Circle, where you'll visit Þingvellir National Park, the Geysir geothermal area, and the Gullfoss waterfall. Some tours also include a visit to the Secret Lagoon or the Kerid crater. Check out Reykjavik Excursions or Gray Line Iceland.
- **South Coast Tours:** Explore the beautiful south coast with its waterfalls, black sand beaches, and bird cliffs. Many tours also include a visit to the Jökulsárlón glacier lagoon. Have a look at Extreme Iceland for tour options.
- **Whale Watching and Puffin Tours:** Departing from the Old Harbour, these tours offer a chance to see whales, dolphins, and puffins in their natural habitat. Elding Whale Watching and Special Tours are two reliable operators.
- **Northern Lights Tours:** Between September and April, a variety of tour operators offer guided trips to chase the northern lights. This unforgettable experience is a must-do for any winter visitor. Try SuperJeep Northern Lights Hunt.
- **Food and Beer Tours:** For a different perspective, consider a food or beer tour to learn more about Icelandic cuisine and craft beer. Check out Wake Up Reykjavik for options.

- **Glacier and Volcano Tours:** For the adventurous, tours to glaciers and volcanoes, including ice cave tours and glacier hikes, are offered by several companies, such as Arctic Adventures.

Always remember to book in advance, especially during peak travel seasons, to ensure availability. Also, keep in mind that the Icelandic weather is unpredictable and tours might be cancelled due to adverse conditions. Always check the weather forecast and make sure to dress accordingly.

6. Shopping

Reykjavik offers a variety of shopping experiences, from modern malls and trendy boutiques to local markets and specialty shops. Here's a guide to help you find the perfect Icelandic souvenir or the latest Nordic fashion trend.

6.1 Shopping Centers and Malls

- **Kringlan Mall:** This is the largest shopping mall in Reykjavik, with over 180 stores, restaurants, and services, including a cinema. Website: Kringlan Mall

- **Smáralind Mall:** Located in the neighboring town of Kópavogur, Smáralind is another large shopping center with a wide range of shops and restaurants. Website:

6.2 Local Markets

- **Kolaportið Flea Market:** Open on weekends, this indoor flea market is the perfect place to hunt for vintage clothing, second-hand books, vinyl records, and more. Don't forget to try the traditional Icelandic fermented shark!

- **Farmers Market:** While not a traditional farmers market, this is actually a popular Icelandic clothing brand known for its quality and design. They have a flagship store in the city. Website: Farmers Market

6.3 Souvenir and Specialty Shops

- **The Handknitting Association of Iceland:** This is the place to find traditional Icelandic woolen goods, including the famous lopapeysa sweaters. Website: The Handknitting Association of Iceland

- **Mál og Menning Bookstore:** A great place to pick up Icelandic literature, whether you're looking for sagas in English or contemporary Icelandic novels.

6.4 Icelandic Design and Fashion Stores

- **Geysir:** One of the most popular fashion brands in Iceland, they offer clothing inspired by the Icelandic environment and lifestyle. Website: Geysir

- **Aurum by Guðbjörg:** An Icelandic jewelry designer known for her nature-inspired designs. Website: Aurum

- **Húsavík Original Whale Watching and Puffin Store:** This store offers eco-friendly products, including their own brand of outdoor clothing designed for whale watching. Website: Húsavík Store

Remember, Iceland's VAT is 24%, but tourists can get a refund at the airport for purchases over 6,000 ISK from shops that participate in the tax-free shopping scheme. Look for the "Tax-Free Shopping" sign when you're out shopping.

7. Nightlife

Reykjavik may be a small city, but its nightlife scene is impressively vibrant and diverse. From sophisticated cocktail bars and historic pubs to bustling clubs and live music venues, there's something for every night owl.

7.1 Clubs and Live Music Venues

- **Húrra:** This is a popular downtown bar and concert venue, known for hosting live music of all genres. From jazz and indie to hip hop and electronica, Húrra is a key player in Reykjavik's music scene. Address: Tryggvagata 22, 101 Reykjavík

- **Gaukurinn:** A rock bar and music venue that hosts regular concerts, including the popular Drag-Súgur drag show. They have a wide selection of beers and an inclusive, friendly atmosphere. Address: Tryggvagata 22, 101 Reykjavík

- **Kaffibarinn:** This bar/club, partly owned by Damon Albarn of Blur and Gorillaz fame, is a hot spot in Reykjavik's nightlife and often features DJ sets on the weekends. Address: Bergstaðastræti 1, 101 Reykjavík

7.2 Pubs and Bars

- **Micro Bar:** If you're interested in trying local Icelandic beer, Micro Bar has one of the largest selections in the city. They offer a constantly changing selection of craft beers from around Iceland. Address: Vesturgata 2, 101 Reykjavík

- **Lebowski Bar:** A fun and casual bar themed around the film The Big Lebowski, it's a great place to relax and enjoy a burger with your White Russian. Address: Laugavegur 20b, 101 Reykjavík

- **Slippbarinn:** Located in the Icelandair Hotel Reykjavik Marina, Slippbarinn is considered the pioneer of the Reykjavik cocktail scene. It's a great spot for a sophisticated drink. Address: Mýrargata 2, 101 Reykjavík

The nightlife in Reykjavik starts late and ends in the early morning hours, especially on weekends. It's also quite common for people to start the night at home before heading out around midnight. And remember, always drink responsibly. Iceland has strict drink-driving laws, with virtually zero tolerance.

7.3 Cultural Performances and Shows

Reykjavik boasts a thriving arts scene, with numerous venues for theater, dance, opera, and more. Here are some highlights:

- **Harpa Concert Hall and Conference Centre:** A stunning piece of architecture on the Reykjavik harbor, Harpa is home to the Iceland Symphony Orchestra and the Icelandic Opera. It also hosts a variety of other performances and events throughout the year. Check their schedule on their website: Harpa

- **National Theatre of Iceland:** Hosting a variety of plays, musicals, and dance performances, the National Theatre offers both contemporary and classical productions. Website: National Theatre

- **Reykjavík City Theatre:** This is another major venue for theatre and dance performances. They occasionally have performances with English subtitles.

7.4 Festivals and Events

Reykjavik hosts several major festivals and events throughout the year, attracting both local and international attendees:

- **Iceland Airwaves (November):** This annual music festival showcases both established and up-and-coming Icelandic bands, as well as international acts. It's one of the premier events for discovering new music. Website: Iceland Airwaves

- **Reykjavík Pride (August):** A colorful and vibrant event, Reykjavík Pride celebrates the LGBTQ+ community with a week of events culminating in a large parade and outdoor concert. Website: Reykjavík Pride

- **Reykjavik International Film Festival (September-October):** A diverse selection of films from around the globe are showcased during this annual festival. Website: RIFF

- **Culture Night (August):** Known as 'Menningarnótt', this annual event marks the end of the summer. It includes numerous cultural events, outdoor concerts, and fireworks, attracting up to a third of the entire population of Iceland.

These events not only provide entertainment but also a unique insight into the vibrant and creative culture of Reykjavik.

8. Outdoor Activities and Adventure

Reykjavik's surrounding landscapes offer a wealth of opportunities for outdoor adventures, from hiking and wildlife watching to water sports and more.

8.1 Hiking and Walking Trails

- **Mount Esja:** The mountain range located just outside of Reykjavik offers several hiking trails with varying difficulty levels. The view from the top over Reykjavik and the surrounding bay is breathtaking.

- **Heiðmörk Nature Reserve:** This beautiful reserve, located on the outskirts of Reykjavik, offers many walking and cycling paths through lush woodland, lava formations, and around a peaceful lake.

- **Reykjavik City Walking Tour:** For a more urban exploration, consider a self-guided walking tour around Reykjavik's city center. This is a great way to discover the city's historic sites, vibrant street art, and hidden gems.

8.2 Water Sports

- **Surfing:** Believe it or not, surfing is possible in Iceland! Cold water surfing is a unique experience, with waves available for all levels. Adventure Vikings offers surfing tours for beginners and experienced surfers alike. Website: Adventure Vikings

- **Kayaking:** Explore the coastal areas of Reykjavik by sea kayak. A variety of companies offer guided kayak tours, allowing you to experience the city from a different perspective.

8.3 Whale and Puffin Watching

- **Whale Watching:** Iceland is one of the best places in the world for whale watching. Companies like Elding and Special Tours offer tours leaving from Reykjavik's Old Harbour. There's a good chance of seeing minke whales, humpback whales, harbor porpoises, and even orcas.

- **Puffin Watching:** In summer, you can take a boat trip from the Old Harbour to the nearby islands, which are home to thousands of puffins. It's a great opportunity to see these charming birds up close.

8.4 Northern Lights Viewing

The Northern Lights, or Aurora Borealis, is one of the most sought-after experiences in Iceland. Although they are a natural phenomenon and sightings can never be guaranteed, the dark, clear skies of Iceland's winter months (September to mid-April) offer some of the best opportunities to see them.

- **In the City:** Despite its status as a capital city, light pollution in Reykjavik is relatively low, and it's possible to see the Northern Lights even within city limits. Places like the Grotta Lighthouse provide a darker setting without leaving the city.

- **Guided Tours:** Many companies offer Northern Lights tours, which usually involve a guide driving you out into the countryside away from city lights. Examples include Gray Line and Reykjavik Excursions. Some tours even offer a second chance for free if you don't see the lights on your first attempt.

- **On Your Own:** If you have a rental car, you can chase the lights yourself. Keep an eye on the aurora forecast on the Icelandic Met Office's website: Icelandic Met Office.

Remember to dress warmly—the Icelandic winter nights can be very cold, especially if you are standing still outside for a while waiting for the lights to appear!

8.5 Hot Springs and Geothermal Pools

Iceland is known for its geothermal activity, and soaking in a hot spring or geothermal pool is a quintessential Icelandic experience.

Blue Lagoon:

Iceland's most famous geothermal spa, located between Reykjavik and Keflavik Airport. It can get quite busy, so book in advance. Website: Blue Lagoon

Reykjavik's City Pools: There are several geothermal pools in Reykjavik itself, where both locals and visitors alike enjoy soaking. Laugardalslaug is the largest, but Vesturbæjarlaug in the west town has a charming local vibe.

Secret Lagoon: Located a bit further out in the Golden Circle area, this is a smaller and less touristy option compared to the Blue Lagoon. Website: Secret Lagoon

Don't forget to shower without a swimsuit before entering the pools—it's an Icelandic rule in the name of hygiene!

9. Health and Safety

Iceland is known as one of the safest countries in the world, and Reykjavik is no exception. However, it's always good to know what health and safety resources are available.

9.1 Health and Medical Facilities

Iceland has an excellent healthcare system, and there are several medical facilities in Reykjavik:

- **Landspítali - The National University Hospital of Iceland:** This is the main hospital in Reykjavik, providing a wide range of services. It has two locations: Fossvogur (Fossvogur, 108 Reykjavík) and Hringbraut (Hringbraut, 101 Reykjavík).

- **Primary Health Care of the Capital Area:** This organization operates several health clinics around the city for non-emergency medical care. Website: Healthcare.is

- **Pharmacies:** There are numerous pharmacies (or "Apótek") throughout the city. Lyfja and Apótek are two of the main chains.

If you're a European Union citizen, remember to bring your European Health Insurance Card (EHIC). Non-EU visitors should ensure they have appropriate travel health insurance.

9.2 Safety Tips and Emergency Numbers

Despite its reputation as a safe city, standard precautions should still be taken. Avoid walking alone late at night in deserted areas and keep an eye on your belongings in crowded places.

The emergency number in Iceland is **112**. This number can be dialed for any kind of emergency, whether it's a health issue, a crime, or an accident.

When exploring outdoors, always respect safety signs and stay on marked trails. The weather in Iceland can change rapidly, so check the forecast before heading out and make sure you're dressed appropriately.

9.3 Accessibility for Travelers with Disabilities

Reykjavik has made significant strides in becoming more accessible for travelers with disabilities. Many public spaces and tourist attractions, including Harpa Concert Hall and most museums, are wheelchair accessible.

Most sidewalks in the city center have curb cuts, and a growing number of restaurants, shops, and hotels have accessible entrances. Larger hotels often have rooms specifically designed for wheelchair users.

For those with visual or hearing impairments, the Icelandic Association of the Deaf and the Icelandic Association of the Visually Impaired can provide resources and assistance.

Several companies offer accessible tours for visitors with mobility impairments, such as Iceland Unlimited.

In general, it's recommended to contact places or tour operators in advance to ensure they can meet your specific needs.

10. Travel Tips and Cultural Etiquette

Understanding a bit about Icelandic culture, etiquette, and practicalities can greatly enhance your visit to Reykjavik.

10.1 Currency, Credit Cards, and Tipping

The currency in Iceland is the Icelandic króna (ISK). While you can find ATMs and currency exchange offices in Reykjavik, most transactions in Iceland are done by card, even for small amounts. It's advisable to have a chip-enabled credit or debit card for your trip. Visa and MasterCard are widely accepted.

Tipping is not a custom in Iceland, as service charges are included in the bill. However, if you receive exceptional service and want to leave a tip, it will not be refused.

10.2 Internet and Connectivity

Reykjavik is well-connected, with free Wi-Fi available in many hotels, cafes, and public spaces. However, if you plan on doing a lot of traveling outside the city or need consistent internet access, consider purchasing a local SIM card from providers such as Siminn or Vodafone. They offer prepaid data packages and can be purchased at the airport or various locations throughout the city.

10.3 Cultural Norms and Etiquette

Icelanders are known for their friendliness and hospitality, but they also value their personal space. When meeting someone, a simple handshake is the norm. Also, Icelanders generally use first names, even in formal settings.

Icelanders have a strong respect for nature. When exploring, make sure to stay on marked paths, don't litter, and don't disturb wildlife or natural formations.

If you're visiting a swimming pool or a hot spring, note that you're expected to shower naked before entering the pool. This is a standard hygiene practice in Iceland and is strictly enforced.

10.4 Icelandic Language Basics

While nearly all Icelanders speak excellent English, it's always appreciated when visitors make an effort to learn a few words in Icelandic. Familiarizing yourself with some basic Icelandic phrases can enhance your cultural experience and create a positive connection with the locals. Here are a few essentials to get you started:

- **Hello**: Halló or Góðan dag (Good day) - Use "Halló" for a casual greeting, and "Góðan dag" for a more formal or polite approach.

- **Thank you**: Takk - Express your gratitude with a simple "Takk." Icelanders appreciate politeness, and a heartfelt "Takk" goes a long way.

- **Yes**: Já - Use "Já" to affirm or agree with something. It's a straightforward and universal word.

- **No**: Nei - "Nei" is the word for "no." It's handy for indicating your preference or declining something politely.

- **Please**: Vinsamlegast - When making a request or asking for assistance, adding "Vinsamlegast" (pronounced vin-sahm-leh-gahst) before or after your sentence is a courteous way to express politeness.

- **Goodbye:** Bless - "Bless" is the common way to say goodbye in Icelandic. It's a warm and friendly farewell.

- **Excuse me/Sorry**: Afsakið - If you need to get someone's attention or apologize, use "Afsakið" (pronounced ahf-sah-kid). It can be used to politely excuse yourself in various situations.

Remember, Icelandic is a unique language with its own pronunciation and grammar. Don't worry too much about perfect pronunciation - Icelanders understand the challenges of their language and appreciate any effort made by visitors to communicate in Icelandic. Even if you stumble, the locals will likely respond in English and be delighted by your attempt.

To delve further into the Icelandic language, consider using language-learning apps or phrasebooks. These resources can provide additional vocabulary, phrases, and pronunciation guides to enhance your language skills.

So, embrace the opportunity to learn a few Icelandic phrases and immerse yourself in the local culture. Your efforts will be met with appreciation and may lead to meaningful connections with the people you meet during your time in Reykjavik.

11. Seasonal Guide

Reykjavik, like the rest of Iceland, experiences dramatic changes between its seasons. Here's a breakdown of what to expect in each season, and tips on how to plan accordingly.

11.1 Summer in Reykjavik

Summer (June to August) is the peak tourist season in Reykjavik. The city enjoys the midnight sun, with almost 24 hours of daylight at the summer solstice. Average temperatures range between 10-15°C (50-59°F), but can occasionally rise to around 20°C (68°F).

This is an ideal time for outdoor activities like hiking, whale watching, and exploring the city's many parks and green spaces. It's also the time for outdoor festivals, such as the Secret Solstice music festival, and cultural events.

Remember to bring a sleep mask if you're sensitive to light when sleeping. Despite the long days, do not underestimate the power of the sun and use sunscreen when outdoors.

11.2 Winter in Reykjavik

Winter (November to March) in Reykjavik is characterized by shorter days—with only about four to five hours of daylight at the winter solstice—and colder weather, with temperatures usually below freezing. Snow is common and can add to the city's charm.

This is the best time to try and catch the Northern Lights, and there are many tours available that will take you out of the city for the best viewing opportunities. Winter is also a great time for enjoying cozy cafes and cultural attractions, like museums and galleries, or relaxing in one of the city's many geothermal pools.

Dressing in layers is key during winter, and waterproof shoes are a must.

11.3 Best Time to Visit

The best time to visit Reykjavik depends largely on your preferences and what you want to do. If you're interested in outdoor activities, festivals, and long days of exploration, then summer is the best time for you. If you want to see the Northern Lights, enjoy winter activities, or prefer fewer tourists, then winter would be your best choice.

Spring (April to June) and fall (September to October) can be excellent times to visit as well, offering a balance between the extreme light conditions of winter and summer, fewer tourists, and generally milder weather.

Regardless of when you visit, Reykjavik is a city that offers vibrant culture, rich history, and beautiful landscapes all year round.

12. Itineraries

12.1 One-day Itinerary

Let's get the most out of your one day in Reykjavik, from dawn till dusk.

7:00 AM: Breakfast at Reykjavik Roasters

Start your day off right with a hearty breakfast at Reykjavik Roasters (Website), one of the city's most beloved coffee shops. Enjoy freshly roasted coffee and a selection of pastries. Price: Around 1,500 ISK.

Address: Kárastígur 1, 101 Reykjavík

8:00 AM: Morning Walk around Tjörnin

Take a peaceful morning walk around Tjörnin, a beautiful city pond just a short stroll from Reykjavik Roasters. It's a popular spot among locals, where you'll see numerous birds, including ducks, geese, and swans.

9:00 AM: Visit Hallgrímskirkja Church

Head to the Hallgrímskirkja Church (Website), an iconic landmark of Reykjavik. Its unique design is inspired by Iceland's natural landscapes. Take the elevator to the top of the tower for a panoramic view of the city. Price: 1,000 ISK.

Address: Hallgrímstorg 1, 101 Reykjavík

10:30 AM: Explore the Reykjavik Art Museum

Visit the Reykjavik Art Museum (Website), located in three separate buildings. We recommend starting with Hafnarhús, located near the old harbour, which houses contemporary art. Price: 1,600 ISK.

Address: Tryggvagata 17, 101 Reykjavík

12:30 PM: Lunch at Fish Market

Enjoy a lunch of fresh, local seafood at Fish Market (Website). Try their "Taste of Iceland" menu for a variety of Icelandic flavors. Price: 7,900 ISK for the tasting menu.

Address: Aðalstræti 12, 101 Reykjavík

2:00 PM: Visit the National Museum of Iceland

After lunch, head to the National Museum of Iceland (Website), which provides a comprehensive overview of Iceland's history and culture. Price: 2,000 ISK.

Address: Suðurgata 41, 101 Reykjavík

4:00 PM: Explore Laugavegur Street

Spend the afternoon exploring Laugavegur Street, the main shopping street in Reykjavik. Here you'll find a range of shops from high-end boutiques to quirky local stores.

6:00 PM: Relax at the Blue Lagoon

Take a 40-minute bus ride from Reykjavik to the Blue Lagoon (Website). It's a geothermal spa known for its milky-blue seawater. Remember to book in advance. Standard entry starts at 6,990 ISK.

Address: Nordurljosavegur 9, 240 Grindavík

9:00 PM: Dinner at Grillmarkaðurinn

Return to the city and end your day with a delicious dinner at Grillmarkaðurinn (Website), a high-end grill that serves Icelandic meats and seafood.

12.2 Three-day Itinerary

The following three-day itinerary will allow you to experience the best of Reykjavik while also exploring some of the natural wonders just outside the city.

Day 1: Exploring Reykjavik City

Morning:

Start your day with a hearty breakfast at Sandholt Bakery, known for their freshly baked breads and pastries.

After breakfast, visit the iconic Hallgrímskirkja Church and enjoy the stunning city view from the top of its tower.

Next, stroll along Skólavörðustígur Street to Laugavegur, the main shopping street in Reykjavik.

Afternoon:

Grab lunch at Cafe Loki, a traditional Icelandic restaurant located across the street from Hallgrímskirkja.

Post lunch, head to Harpa Concert Hall to admire the stunning architecture and if possible, catch a performance.

End your afternoon at the Old Harbor area where you can explore the Maritime Museum or the Saga Museum.

Evening:

For dinner, try Fish Market or Grillmarkaðurinn for high-quality Icelandic cuisine.

After dinner, if you're up for a drink, visit one of Reykjavik's bars. Kaffibarinn, Lebowski Bar, and Micro Bar are popular options.

Day 2: Golden Circle Tour

Morning to Afternoon:

On your second day, embark on a tour of the Golden Circle, a popular route that includes three major attractions: Thingvellir National Park, Geysir Geothermal Area, and Gullfoss Waterfall. Many tour companies operate these tours, such as Reykjavik Excursions and Gray Line Iceland.

Evening:

Return to Reykjavik in the late afternoon and enjoy a casual dinner at Saeta Svinid Gastropub or try the famous Icelandic hot dogs at Bæjarins Beztu Pylsur.

Day 3: South Coast and Relaxation

Morning to Afternoon:

On the final day, take a tour to the South Coast of Iceland, which usually includes Seljalandsfoss and Skógafoss waterfalls, the black sand beach of Reynisfjara, and the small town of Vík.

Evening:

Return to Reykjavik and unwind at the Blue Lagoon geothermal spa, which is the perfect way to relax after a full day of sightseeing.

For your final dinner in Reykjavik, book a table at Dill Restaurant, the first restaurant in Iceland to receive a Michelin star, to sample some innovative Nordic cuisine.

Please note: It's recommended to book tours and dinner reservations in advance. Also, remember to check the weather forecast before planning outdoor activities as weather in Iceland can be unpredictable.

12.3 One-week Itinerary

A week in and around Reykjavik gives you a fantastic opportunity to immerse yourself in the city's culture while also exploring Iceland's breathtaking natural landscapes. Here's a proposed itinerary.

Day 1: Reykjavik City Tour

Start your week with a day exploring Reykjavik. Visit the Hallgrímskirkja Church, take a walk along Laugavegur shopping street, and explore the Old Harbor area. End your day with dinner at a local restaurant like Grillmarkaðurinn.

Day 2: Golden Circle Tour

Spend the second day on the Golden Circle tour, which includes Thingvellir National Park, Geysir Geothermal Area, and Gullfoss Waterfall. Return to Reykjavik for dinner.

Day 3: South Coast Tour

On the third day, take a tour to the South Coast of Iceland. Highlights include Seljalandsfoss and Skógafoss waterfalls, Reynisfjara black sand beach, and Vík town.

Day 4: Museums and Art Galleries

Spend the fourth day delving into Icelandic history and culture at the National Museum of Iceland, Reykjavik Art Museum, and the Saga Museum. Enjoy dinner at one of Reykjavik's culinary hotspots, such as Fish Market.

Day 5: Whale Watching and Puffin Tour

Embark on a whale watching and puffin tour from Reykjavik's Old Harbor. Spend your evening exploring the city's nightlife scene.

Day 6: Snaefellsnes Peninsula

Take a day trip to the beautiful Snaefellsnes Peninsula, often referred to as "Iceland in miniature" due to the variety of landscapes you can see here, including mountains, black sand beaches, and the famous Kirkjufell mountain.

Day 7: Blue Lagoon and Farewell Dinner

Spend your last day relaxing at the Blue Lagoon before enjoying a farewell dinner at a top-rated restaurant, such as Dill Restaurant.

Please remember to book tours and dinner reservations in advance. Also, always check the weather forecast before planning outdoor activities, as Iceland's weather can be unpredictable. It's also recommended to rent a car for maximum flexibility, particularly for the Snaefellsnes Peninsula trip.

12.4 Special Interest Itineraries

Reykjavik and its surrounding regions offer an array of activities for individuals with specific interests. Here are a few ideas:

12.4.1 Nature and Wildlife Lover's Itinerary

Day 1: Start with a city tour of Reykjavik, focusing on the city's green spaces like the Reykjavik Botanical Gardens and the city pond, Tjörnin.

Day 2: Embark on a Golden Circle tour to experience some of Iceland's most breathtaking natural wonders.

Day 3: Take a whale-watching tour from Reykjavik's Old Harbor and visit the Family Park and Zoo to meet some local Icelandic animals.

Day 4: Head out to the South Coast for stunning waterfalls, black sand beaches, and bird watching at Dyrhólaey.

Day 5: Explore Heiðmörk Nature Reserve, a haven for hiking and horse riding.

12.4.2 Foodie's Itinerary

Day 1: Start with a tour of Reykjavik's best bakeries and coffee shops. Take a cooking class in the evening to learn about traditional Icelandic cuisine.

Day 2: Spend the day exploring Reykjavik's local food markets, such as Kolaportið Flea Market.

Day 3: Book a food tasting tour that will take you around the city to sample the best of Icelandic cuisine.

Day 4: Visit the Grandi Food Hall, and later take part in a beer tasting tour at a local brewery.

Day 5: Head out to the South Coast and include a visit to a local farm for a truly farm-to-table experience.

12.4.3 Art and Culture Lover's Itinerary

Day 1: Visit the Reykjavik Art Museum, National Gallery of Iceland, and the Einar Jónsson Museum.

Day 2: Explore the city's street art and design shops on Laugavegur and Skólavörðustígur streets.

Day 3: Take part in a workshop or class, such as a traditional knitting workshop or a sagas storytelling session.

Day 4: Attend a performance at Harpa Concert Hall and explore the Maritime Museum in the Old Harbor area.

Day 5: Explore the museums and cultural institutions of Reykjavik University and the National Museum of Iceland.

Please remember that many museums, performances, and workshops may require advance booking, and availability may be affected by local holidays or other closures. Always check ahead.

13. Beyond Reykjavik

While Reykjavik is a fascinating city to explore, Iceland's true charm lies in its stunning natural beauty, much of which is located just beyond the city limits. One of the best ways to witness this is through the popular tourist route known as the Golden Circle. This approximately 300-kilometer loop takes you through some of the country's most famous natural wonders, including Thingvellir National Park, the Geysir Geothermal Area, and the Gullfoss Waterfall.

13.1 Golden Circle

The Golden Circle route starts and ends in Reykjavik, making it an excellent day trip option. The entire trip, including stops, typically takes between 7-8 hours, depending on how long you choose to spend at each location. Here is a breakdown of the main sites you'll encounter:

1. Thingvellir National Park (Þingvellir)

The first stop on the Golden Circle is Thingvellir National Park, a UNESCO World Heritage site located about 49 kilometers northeast of Reykjavik. The drive takes approximately 45-60 minutes via Route 36.

This vast, open park is of immense historical, cultural, and geological significance. It was the site of Iceland's first parliament, the Alþingi, established by the Vikings in the year 930 AD, making it one of the oldest parliamentary institutions in the world. It's also a geologically fascinating site as it lies in a rift valley caused by the separation of two tectonic plates.

53

There are several walking trails throughout the park, and one of the highlights is the Öxarárfoss waterfall. Diving enthusiasts may want to try Silfra, a unique diving spot located between the North American and Eurasian tectonic plates.

Admission to the park is free, but there is a parking fee of ISK 750.

2. Geysir Geothermal Area

The next stop is the Geysir Geothermal Area, located 60 kilometers east of Thingvellir or about a 60-minute drive via Routes 365 and 37. This active geothermal field features bubbling mud pools, steam vents, and two famous geysers: Geysir and Strokkur.

While Geysir is now mostly dormant, Strokkur erupts regularly every 6-10 minutes, shooting water up to 30 meters into the air. The Geysir Center nearby offers exhibitions and a restaurant.

Entrance to the Geysir Geothermal Area is free of charge.

3. Gullfoss Waterfall

Only a 10-minute drive (9.5 kilometers) northeast of Geysir along Route 35 lies your final primary stop: the majestic Gullfoss Waterfall. Gullfoss, which translates to "Golden Falls," is one of Iceland's most iconic and beloved waterfalls.

The waterfall consists of two distinct cascades, dropping a total of 32 meters into a deep, narrow canyon. There are several viewing platforms offering different perspectives of the falls.

Like the other Golden Circle attractions, there is no admission fee to view Gullfoss, but donations are welcomed in the visitor center, which also houses a cafe and a souvenir shop.

Additional Tips:

While it's possible to complete the Golden Circle route by public bus, having a rental car gives you more flexibility and convenience. Numerous tour companies also offer guided day tours for those who prefer not to drive.

Remember to dress warmly, even in summer, as weather conditions can change rapidly. Waterproof clothing is especially useful at Gullfoss, where the spray from the falls can make you wet.

Always respect the marked paths and safety barriers, especially around the Geysir area, where the ground can be unstable and the water extremely hot.

Other Attractions:

If you have more time and wish to extend your Golden Circle tour, there are several other attractions within a short drive:

- **Kerið Crater Lake:**

This volcanic crater lake located along Route 35 is worth a quick stop. It has a distinctive red and green landscape, making for a beautiful photo opportunity. There is a small entrance fee of ISK 400.

Faxi Waterfall:

Also located along Route 35, this waterfall is less visited than Gullfoss but is still quite beautiful. There's a viewing platform and a picnic area nearby.

- **Secret Lagoon in Flúðir:** If you're looking to relax after a long day of exploring, consider a visit to the Secret Lagoon, a geothermal hot spring located in the small village of Flúðir, just a 30-minute drive from Gullfoss.

- **Friðheimar Tomato Farm:** An excellent place for a lunch stop, this greenhouse farm grows tomatoes all year round and serves tomato-based dishes like soup and bloody marys.

Golden Circle Driving Tips:

Iceland's weather can change rapidly, and even though the Golden Circle roads are well maintained, they can become slippery in rainy or snowy conditions. Always check the weather and road cond"itions before setting off (http://www.road.is/ or https://en.vedur.is/).

Most of the Golden Circle route does not have street lighting, so try to complete the drive during daylight hours, particularly in winter when daylight hours are limited.

In terms of fuel, there are several gas stations in and around Selfoss and Laugarvatn, so make sure to fill up before heading out on the Golden Circle route.

Lastly, while the journey is certainly beautiful, remember to only stop your car in designated parking areas. Not only is this safer, but it's also respectful to local traffic and nature.

With this comprehensive guide, you're now ready to embark on an unforgettable journey around Iceland's famous Golden Circle, witnessing the country's most iconic natural attractions along the way. Enjoy your trip!

13.2 South Coast

Just beyond Reykjavik lies the breathtakingly beautiful South Coast of Iceland, a region known for its diverse natural beauty, from majestic waterfalls and expansive black sand beaches to dramatic sea cliffs teeming with birdlife. The South Coast is perfect for day trips or extended adventures. Here's an itinerary of the main highlights, covering a one-way distance of about 200 kilometers from Reykjavik to Vík.

1. Seljalandsfoss and Gljúfrabúi Waterfalls

Your first stop, about 120 kilometers southeast of Reykjavik along Route 1, is the Seljalandsfoss Waterfall. This spectacular waterfall tumbles 60 meters off a high cliff and is famous for the walking path that leads behind the falls, offering a unique perspective (although you will get wet, so waterproof clothing is recommended).

Just a short walk to the north is the lesser-known Gljúfrabúi waterfall, hidden within a narrow canyon. The entrance to the viewing area can be slippery, so be sure to wear sturdy shoes.

2. Skógafoss Waterfall

Continue east along Route 1 for another 30 kilometers, and you'll reach Skógafoss, one of Iceland's biggest and most impressive waterfalls. It drops 60 meters and spans 25 meters across. Climbing the staircase to the right of the falls offers a panoramic view of the coastline and the plains.

3. Sólheimajökull Glacier

Just a 10-minute drive (about 9.5 kilometers) off Route 1 on Route 221 lies Sólheimajökull, a glacier tongue extending from the main Mýrdalsjökull glacier. Guided glacier walks and ice climbing are offered, but never attempt to go onto the glacier without proper equipment or an experienced guide due to the dangers of crevasses.

4. Reynisfjara Black Sand Beach and Dyrhólaey

Further 20 kilometers along Route 1 will bring you to the town of Vík, but before reaching it, consider stopping at the famous Reynisfjara Black Sand Beach. The beach is known for its distinctive basalt columns, dangerous sneaker waves, and the Reynisdrangar sea stacks visible offshore.

Nearby is the Dyrhólaey promontory, offering panoramic views and a large puffin colony in the summer. However, it's closed during nesting season (mid-May to June).

5. Vík

End your journey in the charming town of Vík, the southernmost village in Iceland. Check out its red-roofed church, explore local shops, or visit the black sand beach right in town.

Additional Tips:

For a day trip, you can turn around in Vík and return to Reykjavik, making for a long but rewarding day. If you plan to continue further east to visit sights like the Jökulsárlón Glacier Lagoon or the Vatnajökull National Park, consider staying overnight in Vík or nearby Kirkjubæjarklaustur.

Always check weather and road conditions on www.road.is and www.vedur.is before setting out, especially in winter.

While there are petrol stations in Selfoss and Vík, fill up before leaving Reykjavik to avoid running out of fuel.

And, of course, respect the local environment. Stick to marked paths, heed warning signs, and never try to drive off-road.

13.3 Westfjords

Tucked away in the northwest corner of Iceland, the Westfjords region is a remote and stunningly beautiful area known for its rugged landscapes, abundant wildlife, and quaint fishing villages. Traveling here requires some planning due to the distances involved and the sometimes challenging road conditions, but the rewards are worth it. Here's a suggested itinerary for exploring the Westfjords.

1. Ísafjörður

After a roughly 450 kilometers journey from Reykjavik, you'll arrive in the region's main town, Ísafjörður. This charming fishing village, set against a backdrop of steep mountains, is an excellent base for your Westfjords adventure. Enjoy the local hospitality, explore the small but engaging Maritime Museum, or take a walk around the harbor.

2. Dynjandi Waterfall

About 75 kilometers south of Ísafjörður is one of the Westfjords' most famous sights: the Dynjandi waterfall. Also known as Fjallfoss, this series of waterfalls stretches over 100 meters high, with the main waterfall spanning 30 meters at its widest. The sight and sound of this cascade tumbling down the mountainside is a spectacle not to be missed.

3. Látrabjarg Cliffs

At the westernmost point of Iceland (and Europe) are the Látrabjarg Cliffs, around 100 kilometers from Dynjandi. These sea cliffs, which stretch for 14 kilometers and rise up to 440 meters high, are home to millions of birds, including puffins, northern gannets, guillemots, and razorbills. The cliffs are accessible from mid-June until August.

4. Rauðasandur Beach

Close to Látrabjarg is Rauðasandur, a red sand beach that stretches for 10 kilometers. This tranquil and relatively secluded spot is a great place to relax and soak in the natural beauty of the Westfjords. Please note that the road down to the beach is steep and gravelly, requiring careful driving.

5. Hot Springs

The Westfjords are home to many natural hot springs, perfect for a soothing soak. One of the most popular is the Hellulaug geothermal pool, located near the town of Flókalundur. For a more modern experience, visit the Krossneslaug pool, located on the shore with a fantastic view of the ocean.

Tips for Traveling in the Westfjords:

The roads in the Westfjords can be narrow and winding, with many gravel sections. Always check road conditions on www.road.is before setting out and remember that in this remote region, services can be sparse. Fill up on petrol when you can, pack food and water, and make sure you have a spare tire.

Also, please respect the environment by sticking to marked trails and not disturbing wildlife or vegetation. This region is a paradise for nature lovers, and it's important to help keep it that way.

With its dramatic landscapes and remote charm, the Westfjords offer a unique and unforgettable Icelandic experience. Whether you're exploring picturesque fishing villages, soaking in hot springs, or bird-watching at Látrabjarg, you're sure to fall in love with this stunning region.

13.4 The Icelandic Highlands

The Icelandic Highlands, or "Hálendið" in Icelandic, is a vast, uninhabited region of stark beauty that covers the interior of Iceland. It's a land of rhyolite mountains, geothermal areas, lava fields, black deserts, and powerful rivers. As most roads in the Highlands are only passable during the summer months, and only with a suitable 4x4 vehicle, it's essential to plan your trip carefully. Here's a suggested itinerary for this wild and remote area.

1. Landmannalaugar

Starting from Reykjavik, a 188-kilometer drive along the F208 will lead you to the geothermal wonderland of Landmannalaugar. Here you'll find colorful rhyolite mountains, vast lava fields, and natural hot springs perfect for a dip. Landmannalaugar is also the starting point of the famous Laugavegur hiking trail. Overnight camping is available, but due to the sensitive nature of the area, you are encouraged to use designated camping spots.

2. Hveravellir

From Landmannalaugar, you can head north to Hveravellir along the Kjölur highland road (F35), a journey of about 150 kilometers. Hveravellir is a stunning geothermal area located between two glaciers, Langjökull and Hofsjökull. It features bubbling hot springs, colorful silica deposits, and a geothermal pool for bathing.

3. Askja and Viti Crater

Another spectacular location in the Highlands is the Askja Caldera and the nearby Viti Crater, in the northeast of Iceland. Reaching these requires a long drive from Myvatn (about 150 kilometers) along the F88 and F910. Askja is a large caldera filled with water, known as Öskjuvatn, the second deepest lake in Iceland. Nearby, the Viti Crater contains a geothermal lake of warm, blue water. However, bathing here is not advised due to the unpredictable nature of the geothermal activity.

4. Kerlingarfjöll

Kerlingarfjöll, located in the central highlands between the Kjölur and Sprengisandur routes, is a mountain range known for its geothermal areas and striking red and orange rhyolite peaks. The area is a paradise for hikers, with trails leading through steam vents, around hot springs, and up to mountain summits with panoramic views.

Tips for Traveling in the Icelandic Highlands:

Traveling in the Highlands requires a 4x4 vehicle and experience driving on gravel roads. Always check road conditions on www.road.is and weather conditions on www.vedur.is before you set out. Note that many roads in the Highlands are only open during the summer, generally from late June until September.

There are few services in the Highlands, so be prepared. Fill your fuel tank whenever possible, carry a spare tire, and bring food, water, and warm clothing. There's no mobile phone coverage in many parts of the Highlands, so let someone know your travel plan before you go.

Respect the delicate environment by staying on marked roads and trails, not disturbing wildlife, and taking all trash with you.

The Icelandic Highlands are challenging to access but offer some of the most breathtaking and unique landscapes on the planet. With careful planning and respect for the environment, a journey into the Highlands can be the adventure of a lifetime.

14. Three-Day Detailed Itinerary

1st Day In Reykjavik - Itinerary

9:00

Arrival at Keflavik Airport (KEF)

9:30

Go from the airport to the hotel by Straetó n°55 bus or Flybus transfer. We suggest you stay at a hotel or hostel in Downtown Reykjavik, where you will be able to see most of the city's attractions and lifestyle.

Cost: 13€ - 20 €

10:15

Arrival at the hotel. Check in at the hotel and rest for a while after your flight and before the beginning of your 3-days journey across Reykjavik and its beautiful surroundings.

11:00

Go to a Rental Car Agency. We will prepare this guide considering the option of renting a car for driving yourself to the most incredible Icelandic spots near Reykjavik. If this is not an option because you are traveling alone and it would be too expensive, you can take tours to each one of these places instead. You will find lots of Touristic Centers in downtown Reykjavik that offer these tours and more.

11:30

Now that you have a car, you are ready to begin your journey! Reykjavik is a small city, and you can get to know it in just one day. Moreover, there are many incredible natural spots in its surroundings that you cannot miss by any means. Thus, we will spend the first two days visiting the most famous natural attractions and dedicate the last day of your 3-days holidays in Reykjavik to discover the city itself.

First, **we will go to Thingvellir National Park**, a key location in the history of Iceland. Here it's where the oldest existing parliament in the world was assembled, in 930 AD. Besides this historical significance, the place has a series of natural features and geology that is unique in the world. See *ZoomTip 1.1* to learn more about the **Thingvellir National Park**. The journey from Reykjavik to the Thingvellir National Park takes about 40 minutes driving.

15:00

Keep driving up to **The Great Geysir**. This is without a doubt one of the most famous natural attractions in Iceland. The English word "geyser" is derived from this unique place. The main attraction of the area is The Churn, which is another geyser situated only 100 meters from The Great Geysir that erupts every 10 minutes approximately, and its white column of white boiling water can reach up to 30 meters. See *ZoomTip 1.2* to learn more about **The Great Geysir**. The journey from **Thingvellir National Park** to **The Great Geysi**r takes about 50 minutes driving.

17:00

Now keep driving a bit more up to the **Gullfoss Waterfall**, one of the most iconic and spectacular waterfalls in Iceland. This waterfall is located on the Hvitá river, which is fed by the glacier Langjokull, Iceland's second biggest glacier. See *ZoomTip 1.3* to learn more about this impressively powerful waterfall. The journey from **The Great Geysir** to the **Gullfoss Waterfall** takes just about 10 minutes driving.

18:30

After enjoying this unparalleled beautiful natural spots, **it's time to get back to Reykjavik**. Driving back from the Gullfoss Waterfall to Downtown Reykjavik will take you around 1 hour and a half.

20:30

Go and have dinner at one of the places we suggested in the "Our favorite dining places in Reykjavik" section and think about the amazing and unique places you were lucky to witness during this incredible first day in Iceland while enjoying some of the best local food.

22:00

Get back to the hotel/hostel and get some rest, because another busy day with extraordinary new places to visit will be waiting for you tomorrow.

1st Day in Reykjavik - Map

Below you will find the maps corresponding to all the different places we've recommended for your first day in South Iceland. They are accessible in Google Maps format for you to easily use on your smartphone or tablet while you are in Reykjavik.

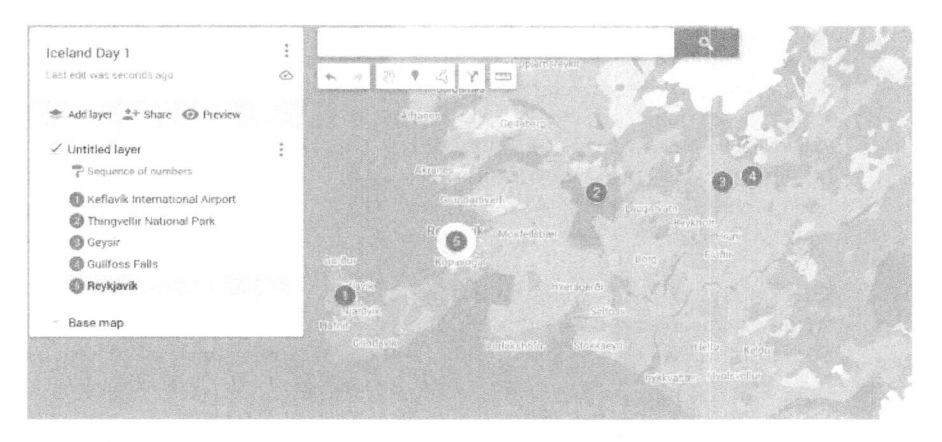

Get this map online:

https://www.google.com/maps/d/edit?mid=1UdeIiQhUzjQ0YgKlrY2bvmGJ41mJ8F8&usp=sharing

ZoomTip 1.1: Thingvellir National Park

The **Thingvellir National Park**, located at 45 km from Reykjavik, is one of the most significant historical places in Iceland. It consists of a total of 237 km² of spectacular natural beauty. The Thingvellir Valley is the visible line that **separates the tectonic plates of North America and Eurasia**. There are two areas where this separation of tectonic plates can be seen best: Almannagjá, which with a total longitude of 7,7 kilometers and a depth that can reach 40 meters clearly shows the separation between the two plates, and Hrafanagjá, which is longer (11 km) but not as deep (30 meters maximum).

A second important aspect of Thingvellir is the fact that **the oldest Parliament in the world was settled here**. The Icelandic Parliament appears in Landnámabók, a book in which the first years of the colonization are described, and the Parliament is dated to the year 874.

The National park is divided into different areas, all of which are very interesting for anyone who would like to walk among virgin territories. On one side you will find an immense lava field, covering the biggest part of the park. There are some trees in the park due to a reforestation process currently occurring, but, as is the case in most Iceland, you will find almost no trees or forests.

ZoomTip 1.2: The Great Geysir

What is known as **The Great Geyser** is the first geyser described in a printed source and the first known geyser in Europe. The word in English "geyser" actually derives from this particular geyser. It has been dormant since 1916, a year in which it suddenly ceased to spout. After that, it only came back to life once in 1935 and immediately went back to sleep. It is a complete mystery whether the silence is definitive or if it will come back to life soon!

The other interesting attraction in this area is, of course, the legendary **Strokkur Geysir**. Every 5 or 10 minutes, the water starts bubbling, and all of a sudden a huge water stream raises up to 30 meters above all of the astonished tourists present at the place. Within a landscape dominated by thermal lakes, black volcanic rocks, and ashes, this majestic geyser comes out as the most significant attraction to those visiting this part of Iceland.

The water comes out to the surface at a temperature of 120 °C, but it does not represent any danger to the tourists since the ambient temperature is so low that it cools the water almost immediately. After this, the water goes back to its usual bubbling state, preparing for the next throw.

It is said that the **Strokkur Geysir** used to be even more spectacular some years ago, reaching heights up to 50 meters, which raises the question if the area becoming a worldwide famous touristic attraction is bringing consequences to the phenomenon.

ZoomTip 1.3: Gullfoss Waterfalls

The impressive **Gullfoss Waterfall** is one of the most visited natural monuments in Iceland, and one of the most impressive waterfalls in Europe, due to its incredible dimensions and the amount of water that it carries. Two major factors explain this. First, the fact that it is a waterfall created by the ruptures that create the Icelandic landscape. An enormous broken rock block has created the waterfall once it moved at some point. This space has been increased through time by the Hvitá River, which means White River. The second primary factor that makes the Gullfoss Waterfall so attractive is its proximity to Reykjavik, making it a must-go for any tourist and part of the most famous touristic route in Iceland, known as "The Golden Circle". The "Golden Circle" includes the **Gullfoss Waterfall**, the **Strokkur Geyser** and the **Thingvellir National Park**.

The arrival at the **Gullfoss Waterfall** is nothing but spectacular, because the terrain hides the course of the river, and since we access the place through the lower side, we can perfectly see the double fracture of the plain on which the Hvitá river comes from, making the impression of the river immerses within the Earth.

The **Gullfoss Waterfall** has been a private property since the middle of the XXth Century, and the possibility of taking advantage of the waterfall for producing electric energy was considered, but the lack of funds made it impossible to continue with this idea.

2nd Day In Reykjavik – Itinerary
9:00

Get some good breakfast, take the car **and go to the Blue Lagoon!** This is another of the most visited and famous attractions in Iceland. It's a geothermal spa, located just 20 km from the Keflavik International Airport and 39 km from downtown Reykjavik. Unlike the other attractions in Iceland that you've visited during your first day, there is an entrance fee to the Blue Lagoon. Prices are dynamic and vary according to the time of day of the visit and how far in advance your ticket is booked, but the minimum price you'll pay is 5500 ISK, which is about 48€. See *ZoomTip 2.1* to learn more about the Blue Lagoon geothermal spa. The journey from downtown Reykjavik to the Blue Lagoon takes about 50 minutes driving.

14:00

After relaxing and enjoying the incredible geothermal spa of Blue Lagoon, it's time to discover the beauty of West Iceland. **Take the car and drive up to Snaefellsjokull National Park.**

This National Park is one of the most visited spots in Iceland and a great place to go if you'd like to get out for a while from the much more touristic area of South Iceland. During your drive up here, you will experiment the characteristic Icelandic loneliness, by finding almost no people on the way. The **Snaefellsjokull Volcano** is by far the biggest attraction in this National Park, and it's where the Jules Verne's Journey to the Center of the Earth novel takes place. Besides this magnificent Volcano, there are other great spots to see this National Park, like black beaches, lava fields or charming little towns, all of which are readily available with your car, so we suggest driving around the whole park and making stops wherever you want to before going back to Reykjavik.

See *ZoomTip 2.2* to learn more about the Snaefellsjokull National Park. The journey from the Blue Lagoon to the Snaefellsjokull National Park takes about 2 hours and a half driving.

19:00

After discovering the beautiful magic of Snaefellsnes and West Iceland, **it's time to get back to Reykjavik!** The journey back to downtown Reykjavik from Snaefellsjokull National Park takes around 2 hours.

21:30

Go back to the hotel and have some dinner. If you're too tired to go and have dinner at some restaurant (or if you feel you're spending too much money by now), you can have some easy meal after buying some groceries at the supermarket.

2nd Day in Reykjavik - Map

Below you will find the maps corresponding to all the different activities that we recommend for your second day in Iceland. They are accessible in Google Maps format for you to easily use on your smartphone or tablet while you are in Reykjavik.

As you can see, now we've covered some big part of West Iceland as well, so you're getting to know this beautiful Iceland during your 3-days visit!

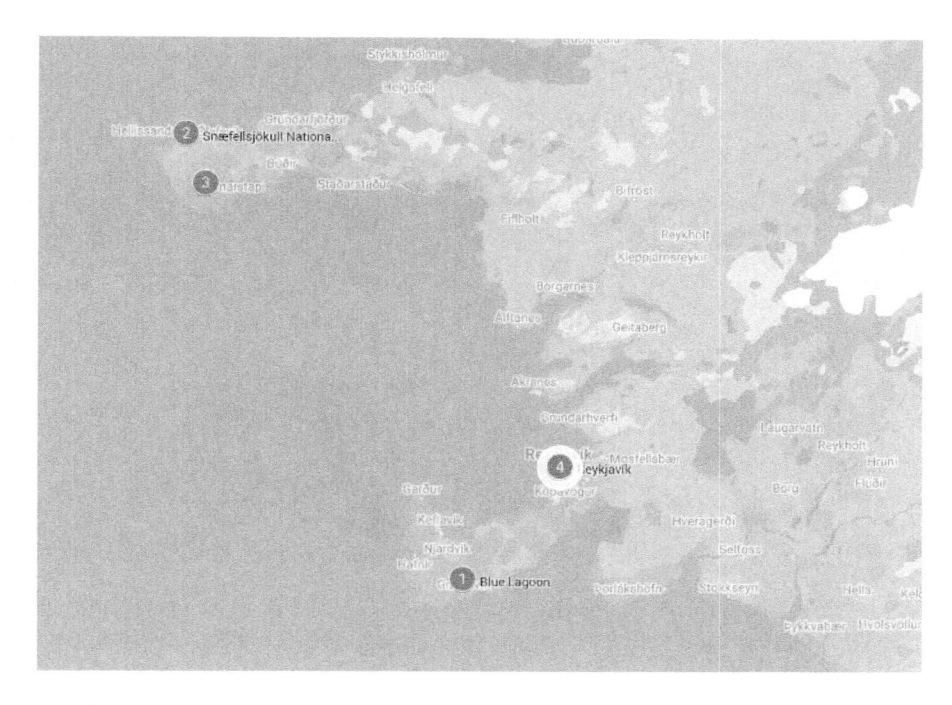

Get this map online:

https://www.google.com/maps/d/edit?mid=1UdeIiQhUzjQoYgKlrY2bvmGJ41mJ8F8&usp=sharing

ZoomTip 2.1: Blue Lagoon geothermal spa

The Blue Lagoon geothermal spa is one of the most visited attractions in Iceland, packed with tourists who are looking to relax and heal in these waters with multiple healing properties. That is because the composition of its geothermal water constitutes a unique mixture of algae ingredients: rich in salt and other minerals, silica and blue algae which give the lake its characteristic color tone.

The **Blue Lagoon** is a geothermal lake situated at the first lava field in West Iceland, about 45 minutes driving from Reykjavik, and near the Keflavik International Airport. *Blaá Lónid*, which is its name in the Icelandic language, was discovered by accident by the end of the 1970's and recognized worldwide for its waters healing properties, especially for the treatment of psoriasis.

It is an artificial lake fed by streams coming from the nearby geothermic central Svartsengi, located 200 meters underground, at a temperature of 240 °C. Due to an incomplete draining of the water coming from the primary, it began to accumulate at this particular place, causing a big surprise to everyone in the area.

In addition to the excellent water healing powers, **the best thing about this place is the stunning landscape**. The contrast between the black volcanic rocks and the bright blue of the water create a unique and unforgettable memory!

There is an entrance fee to be paid for entering the Blue Lagoon, which varies according to the time of the day, the season of the year, and how far in advance you book your ticket. You can find more details on the price on the Blue Lagoon website.

ZoomTip 2.2: Snaefellsjokull National Park

The **Snaefellsjokull National Park** is the only National Park in Iceland that reaches the sea. It is located on the West side of the country, on the Snaefellsnes Peninsula. The park is named after the famous Snaefellsjokull Glacier, which is at the same time a volcano, and once was the entrance point in the Jules Verne's famous novel Journey to the Center of the Earth. Many people believe this place to be one of the seven primary energy spots of Planet Earth. Whether this is true or not, what is not even under discussion is the fact that it is a magnificent place to enjoy fantastic views of the Reykjanes Peninsula, the Western Fjords, and the Snaefellsnes Mountains.

The **Djúpalónssandur Beach** is another fascinating attraction of the Park. It used to be a major fishing port, but nowadays it has ceased its operation. Still, four big rocks are left that were used to measure the strength of the men who wanted to work on the boats: Fullsterkur, of 154 kg, Hálfsterkur, of 100 kg, Hálfdraettingur, of 54 kg and Amlódi, of 23 kg.

By the sea, you will also find two cliffs known as **Lóndrangar**, which are two sharp rocks of 75 and 61 meters high, over which a large variety of birds gather. There is also a beautiful and picturesque lighthouse right next to them.

Other places to visit within the Snaefellsjokull National Park are **the Holaholar Crater**, the **Saxholl Crater**, the **Bardarlaug Natural Swimming Pool** and the **Ytri Tunga Beach**, where a colony of seals lives.

3rd Day In Reykjavik – Itinerary

10:00

Take a walk from the hotel to the Hallgrímskirkja Church. It is an extraordinary and unique construction that will amaze you. It is possible to go up to the tower and have some breathtaking views of the city of Reykjavik. The cost for taking the elevator to go up there is 900 ISK (almost 8€). If you get to the Church by walking through Skólavordustígur Street, you will find lots of beautiful art street decoration, since this street is famous for being the artist's street.

See *ZoomTip 3.1* to learn more about the Hallgrímskirkja Church.

11:30

After seeing the Church and the great views from the tower, **take some time to walk around Reykjavik** (which is not a big city) and watch the locals. The city is picturesque and clean, full of typical nordic little houses. We also suggest you **try the Baejarins Beztu hot dogs**, as we mentioned in the "Our favorite dining places in Reykjavik" section.

14:00

Keep walking towards the Tjornin or Reykjavik Lake area, which is where the Parliament and the City Hall reside. Here at the lake, you will also be able to see hundreds of entire duck families. The lake is one of the best places in Reykjavik to find local people and see how they usually live since the place is usually full of kids with their parents, teenagers and young couples. During the winter, the lake is frozen and used for ice skating.

16:00

Keep walking towards the city port, and you will find tons of little bars and terraces. This is another perfect place to relax and have a drink if you want to. It's also a good place to buy some souvenir for taking back home in case you haven't done it already!

18:00

Get your luggage and head to the airport.

3rd Day in Reykjavik – Map

Below you will find the maps corresponding to all the different activities that we recommend for your third day in Reykjavik. They are accessible in Google Maps format for you to easily use on your smartphone or tablet while you are in Reykjavik.

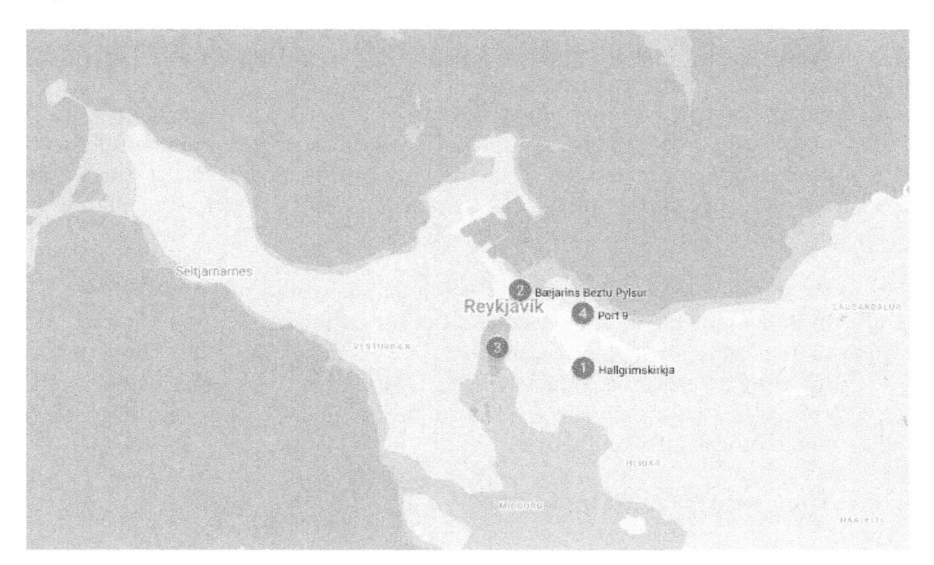

Get this map online:

https://www.google.com/maps/d/edit?mid=1UdeIiQhUzjQ0YgKlrY2bvmGJ41mJ8F8&usp=sharing

ZoomTip 3.1: Hallgrímskirkja Church

Hallgrímskirkja is an iconic landmark and the largest church in Iceland, dominating the skyline of Reykjavik. This striking architectural masterpiece, named after the renowned Icelandic poet and clergyman Hallgrímur Pétursson, is not only a place of worship but also a must-visit attraction for its awe-inspiring design and panoramic views of the city.

Designed by Icelandic architect Guðjón Samúelsson, Hallgrímskirkja is a testament to the unique blend of modern and Gothic architectural styles. Construction began in 1945 and was completed in 1986. The church's most distinctive feature is its towering steeple, reaching a height of 73 meters (244 feet), making it the tallest church in Iceland. The design is said to be inspired by the natural basalt columns found in Icelandic landscapes.

Top Features and Highlights:

1. **The Exterior:** The façade of Hallgrímskirkja is characterized by its stepped concrete columns that ascend towards the sky. The clean lines and minimalist design create a visually striking and contemporary aesthetic.

2. **The Interior:** Step inside the church to experience its serene and minimalist interior. The high vaulted ceiling, elegant columns, and large organ contribute to a sense of grandeur and tranquility. The space is bathed in natural light that filters through the stained glass windows.

3. **The Pipe Organ:** One of the notable features of Hallgrímskirkja is its grand pipe organ, crafted by the renowned German organ builder Johannes Klais. The instrument boasts over 5,200 pipes and is known for its exceptional sound quality.

4. **The Observation Deck:** Ascend the elevator or climb the 86-meter (282-foot) tower for a breathtaking panoramic view of Reykjavik and its surroundings. On clear days, you can even spot distant mountains, the sea, and the colorful rooftops of the city below.

5. **The Statue of Leif Erikson:** In front of the church stands a bronze statue of Leif Erikson, the Icelandic explorer believed to have been the first European to reach North America. The statue is a gift from the United States to Iceland, symbolizing the strong connection between the two countries.

Visiting Hallgrímskirkja:

- **Opening Hours:** The church is open daily, and the opening hours vary depending on the season. Generally, it is open from morning until evening, with shorter hours on Sundays for worship services. The observation deck has separate opening hours.

- **Entry Fee:** Admission to the church is free, but there is a fee to access the observation deck. It costs 900 ISK (almost 8€) to take the elevator that takes you to the top of the tower.

- **Location:** Hallgrímskirkja is located at Hallgrímstorg 1, 101 Reykjavik, Iceland.

Website: www.hallgrimskirkja.is

Hallgrímskirkja stands not only as a place of worship but also as an architectural marvel and a symbol of national pride. Its commanding presence and panoramic views make it a must-visit attraction for any visitor to Reykjavik, offering a unique blend of spiritual solace, cultural appreciation, and awe-inspiring vistas of the city and beyond.

Thank You!

As we conclude our journey through this comprehensive guide to Reykjavik, we hope you've garnered a newfound appreciation for the capital city of Iceland. Reykjavik is a place of compelling contrasts: here, rich history intertwines with vibrant modernity, cosmopolitan life mingles with rugged nature, and long-standing traditions coexist with innovative creativity.

Throughout the city, you'll discover a multitude of experiences waiting to be explored - the historical landmarks steeped in tales from the past, the bustling food and drink scene serving up culinary surprises, the cultural institutions offering an immersion into the Icelandic way of life, and the natural wonders that truly underscore Iceland's epithet as the "Land of Fire and Ice."

This guide is intended as a comprehensive resource to help you plan your journey, but the true essence of Reykjavik is best experienced first-hand. Whether you find yourself basking in the ethereal glow of the Northern Lights, marveling at the intricate architecture of Hallgrímskirkja, indulging in a traditional Icelandic meal, or simply strolling along the colorful streets of the city, you will be partaking in the life and soul of Reykjavik.

Remember, every journey to Reykjavik offers something unique - shaped by the seasons, the people you'll meet, and the path you'll carve for yourself through the city. And therein lies the beauty of travel. It's more than just visiting a destination; it's about the experiences you have, the memories you make, and the stories you bring back.

Enjoy your adventure in Reykjavik, the gateway to the Land of Fire and Ice.

Your friends at Guidora.

Copyright Notice

Guidora Reykjavik in 3 Days Travel Guide ©

All rights reserved. No part of either publication may be reproduced in any material form, including electronic means, without the prior written permission of the copyright owner.

Text and all materials are protected by UK and international copyright and/or trademark law and may not be reproduced in any form except for non-commercial private viewing or with prior written consent from the publisher, with the exception that permission is hereby granted for the use of this material in the form of brief passages in reviews when the source of the quotations is acknowledged.

Disclaimer

The publishers have checked the information in this travel guide, but its accuracy is not warranted or guaranteed. Reykjavik visitors are advised that opening times should always be checked before making a journey.

Tracing Copyright Owners

Every effort has been made to trace the copyright holders of referred material. Where these efforts have not been successful, copyright owners are invited to contact the Editor (Guidora) so that their copyright can be acknowledged and/or the material removed from the publication.

Creative Commons Content

We are most grateful to publishers of Creative Commons material, including images. Our policies concerning this material are (1) to credit the copyright owner, and provide a link where possible (2) to remove Creative Commons material, at once, if the copyright owner so requests - for example, if the owner changes the licensing of an image.

We will also keep our interpretation of the Creative Commons Non-Commercial license under review. Along with, we believe, most web publishers, our current view is that acceptance of the 'Non-Commercial' condition means (1) we must not sell the image or any publication containing the image (2) we may, however, use an image as an illustration for some information which is not being sold or offered for sale.

Note to other copyright owners

We are grateful to those copyright owners who have given permission for their material to be used. Some of the material comes from secondary and tertiary sources. In every case, we have tried to locate the original author or photographer and make the appropriate acknowledgment. In some cases, the sources have proved obscure and we have been unable to track them down. In these cases, we would like to hear from the copyright owners and will be pleased to acknowledge them in future editions or remove the material.

Printed in Great Britain
by Amazon